UNIVERSITY CO

Cost-Benefit Analysis and Public Expenditure

G. H. PETERS

Brunner Professor of Economic Science
University of Liverpool

THIRD EDITION

Published by
THE INSTITUTE OF ECONOMIC AFFAIRS
1973

First published April 1966
Second Edition November 1968
Second Impression August 1969
Third Impression September 1970
Third Edition, revised and enlarged, July 1973
Second Impression November 1974
© THE INSTITUTE OF ECONOMIC AFFAIRS 1966, 1968, 1973

SBN 255 36045-2

Printed in Great Britain by
GORON PRO-PRINT CO. LTD.,
Set in 10 on 12 pt. Times

Contents

Preface to the First Edition

The general purpose of the *Eaton Papers* is to contribute a stream of informative and analytical texts, drawing on the authors' researches, for specialist readers: teachers and students of economics, economists in business, nationalised industries and government, business managers, accountants, investment advisors, lawyers and others. The common theme is the sources and extent of economic information for business and public policy, the restrictions on it and methods of removing them, its scope, interpretation, reliability and limitations.

The better performance of an economy depends not only on increasing the amount of resources and their efficiency in existing uses but also on their better allocation between alternative uses on the basis of decisions made by consumers, firms, public authorities and governments. The quality of these decisions depends in large part on the accuracy and availability of relevant information.

The development of economic analysis has tended to ignore or under-rate the costs of collecting and disseminating information, and the textbook analysis of competitive markets is usually based on the assumption that knowledge is perfect and costless. In a dynamic economy complete knowledge is unobtainable: *ex hypothesi* the conditions of supply and demand are continually changing, and the changes cannot be predicted with a high degree of accuracy because the future is in large part determined by events and decisions that in turn are influenced by information unknown and possibly unknowable in the present. Not least the collection and assimilation of information costs time, money and alternatives sacrificed that may outweigh its value.

In recent years there has been increasing discussion of the information that is thought *not* to be available to (or not *used* by) buyers and sellers engaging in voluntary exchange in the market and the degree to which its absence (or neglect) makes their decisions defective for business or public policy. The argument is that market bargains ignore effects on third parties, both detrimental and beneficial, because they are indirect, 'external', uncovenanted. Some activities are thus over-expanded and others undesirably curtailed. The question is whether it is possible to assemble information on these indirect effects and how they can be taken into account in the market; further, whether a system of taxes and subsidies could limit or enlarge the voluntary bargains of the market place to the point at which they maximise social utility.

The essentials of this proposition were first laid down in 1912 by the late Professor A. C. Pigou in an analysis of what he described as divergences between the ('marginal') private and social net products. Professor R. H. Coase of Chicago, Professor J. M. Buchanan of Virginia, Mr Ralph Turvey and other economists have argued with conviction that some types of divergences between private and social costs or benefits do not adversely affect the efficient use of resources because market decisions can anticipate and avoid them. The inference is that they can be prevented by removing the obstacles to the emergence of market solutions. Professor Jack Wiseman has argued further that the problem is essentially one of deciding on forms of compensation and that the solution lies in revising the laws of property rights. He draws the further inference that many examples of social costs arise from the absence of market pricing, for example in the use of space for roads or car parks.

It would seem that a fundamental weakness of the Pigovian approach is that 'externalities' do not necessarily indicate that the market process frustrates the optimum allocation of resources. The effort to conceive and assess indirect or external effects might rest on an unnecessary assumption about the information available to, or taken into account by, buyers and sellers in the market. It is arguable that third parties should have considered, anticipated and, where practicable, insured against external effects, or at least many of them, and that in practice they do so. A man who buys a house in a town knowingly takes the risk that the house across the road may be painted a disconcerting colour (and the chance that he may benefit from an unexpected bus or underground service). If he moves to the country he knowingly takes the risk that he may lose his view by the erection of houses, gasworks or electricity pylons -(and the chance that he will benefit from an unexpected school, hospital or road). It does not follow he has a claim to be compensated for detriments (or penalised for benefits) he failed to anticipate, or that the activities or property rights of others should be restricted or petrified.

The impact of social costs and benefits on private decisions in the market might therefore be analysed as part of the economic theory of uncertainty, risk and expectations. To some extent the risks are clear enough to be treated as information to take into account in striking voluntary bargains; in other instances they may be insured against; for the rest, they may have to be taken by individuals and accepted as part of the unavoidable costs of voluntary exchange and free bargaining. Where the detriment is so large that the individual cannot protect himself, such as the indirect effects of new dams or major physical engineering works, or the result of capricious 'social (or political) engineering', there may be a case for communal compensation. But the principle applies elsewhere, possibly to long-term unemployment, to civil assault, to massive natural catastrophe by flood or fire, or to war damage. The market has evolved devices for covering large risks by insurance: Lloyds underwrites the risk of loss of a ship by storm or of property by fire. And the market may yet evolve devices to enable individuals by insurance to accept other risks and convert them into known costs; private protection against some at least of the risks covered by the public police forces or fire brigades may conceivably be more flexible, more effective and cheaper. It is not clear that the scope for thus 'internalising' external effects is exhausted, nor that it has been thoroughly explored.

Congestion costs, which form the largest single social detriment in recent discussion, illustrate the underlying difficulties of the concept of 'externality' and its application.

Not only is it impracticable to measure with substantial accuracy the inconvenience and discomfort imposed by motor vehicles on other road users or by public transport passengers on other travellers. In the fundamental economic sense that resources are scarce, every user of a commodity or service of course imposes congestion on other users: a shopper imposes congestion on other shoppers, a holiday-maker on other holiday-makers, a newcomer to a residential town or village on other commuters. The notion of 'congestion' is central to economic theory. And where the effects are demonstrably large and not easily avoidable except in the very long run, there may be a case for *ad hoc,* approximate solutions. But it does not follow that the parties to a voluntary contract who cause social detriment can be or in general should be taxed, or who cause social benefits can be or should be subsidised. Equally it does not imply that third parties who suffer from external defects can be or should be compensated, or who benefit can be or should be penalised. Indirect effects on third parties are probably the inevitable outcome of every act of voluntary purchase or sale. Possibly no decision in the market reflects all costs or all benefits. The market may nevertheless remain the most practicable instrument for registering preferences and allocating resources, either because external costs or benefits cannot be identified or measured or because where they can they are allowed for by sellers and buyers.

It is this precarious concept of externalities in market activities that has been elaborated in the more recent years under various titles, of which 'social cost-benefit theory' seems to be the most common, and applied in varying degrees and forms in Britain and America to town planning, transport and other government services which are not (or, some economists argue, cannot be) supplied in the market. In this *Eaton Paper* Mr G. H. Peters, a young economist at the University of Oxford who has been engaged in research into applications of the theory, reviews it *ab initio* and re-examines its theoretical cohesion and the practical problems of applying it. He reaches conclusions much more sceptical than might be expected from the uncritical re-discovery of the proposition a few years ago and its magnification into a new technique of public policy.

It would seem that the most that can be said for the doctrine is that, by listing the supposed indirect benefits or detriments, it indicates a desire to introduce a semblance of rationality into the spending of large sums by public authority. Mr Peters is doubtful about the extent to which the indirect effects can be measured; he analyses the difficulties in tracing and assessing them and argues that much that pretends to scientific objectivity is little more than subjective value-judgement, if not personal pre-judgement. His analysis suggests that the indirect effects very soon become vague, conjectural, misty, if not mystical. His conclusion is that since probably only a small part of social costs or benefits is measurable, there is little purpose in evaluating them meticulously.

Mr Peters confines himself to analysis without drawing conclusions for public policy. But his scrutiny suggests a further inference. If social cost-benefit theory is defective, it cannot readily be used as an argument for taking decisions out of the market and putting them into the corridors of political power. It is not clear that the social benefits of education, health, housing or other welfare services are sufficiently unambiguous that at least some of these services cannot be arranged voluntarily between individual buyers and sellers but must be provided by political decision through the state. Even if the external effects can be identified it does not follow that the services must be provided by government, only that government should provide finance to individuals to buy them from competiting suppliers and perhaps specify minimum standards until competition becomes vigorous enough to dispense with them.

Mr Peters has written a lucid reappraisal of an economic proposition that has been welcomed as a device for lessening the arbitrariness, inefficiency and uncertainties of state investment. These weaknesses basically remain. Especially when large decisions in town planning, transport, fuel, housing, education, health services, defence and other government departments or services are being made for the next five or more years,[1] his astringent study should stimulate re-thinking and considerably more research before millions of public monies (around two-fifths of national income) are committed irrevocably. It cannot yet be said that the 'economic and social priorities'[1] laid down by government reflect very much more than good intentions or political pressures.

We wish to thank Mr John Brunner, Mr F. G. Pennance of the College of Estate Management, Mr Ralph Turvey, and Professor Wiseman of the University of York for reading and commenting on an early draft of the *Paper*. Like them, the Institute does not necessarily share the author's argument, but offers it as a sobering contribution to public understanding and discussion.

March 1966

EDITOR

---

[1] *Public Expenditure: Planning and Control*, Cmnd. 2915, HMSO, London, February 1966.

Preface to the Third Edition

Among IEA texts that have become widely used by teachers and students of economics, one of the most successful is Professor George Peters's study of cost-benefit analysis and his discussion of the leading literature. The First Edition in 1966 was quickly followed by the Second in 1968, reprinted in 1969 and 1970.

The First Edition filled a gap in the economic appraisal of the increasing volume of writings on what was not essentially a new idea but a development of a proposition that goes back at least as far as Professor A. C. Pigou's *Economics of Welfare*: that voluntary exchanges and contracts in the market could have effects on other parties, beneficial or detrimental. In the last dozen years this notion has flowered into blooms under several names—from social cost/benefit through spillover effects to 'externalities'.

The applications have extended from the early example of factory smoke to the recent and comprehensive debate on environmental pollution. For economists interest fastens on how far externalities can be 'internalised', infelicitous phraseology that nevertheless neatly indicates the task of devising techniques that will make the creators of third party effects bear the costs in the market, and how far other measures are required outside the market. The essentials of the subject are surveyed and the main writings reviewed in the Third Edition of this *Paper*, in which Professor Peters has extensively revised and amplified to include discussion of the most recent example, the proposals for the third London airport. Not only teachers and students of economics, but also people in industry and government, will find the Third Edition a comprehensive though still concise introduction to a large and wide-ranging subject.

June 1973 EDITOR

The Author

G. H. PETERS, M.SC. (ECON.), M.A., was born in North Wales in 1934. He studied economics at the University College, Aberystwyth, and at Cambridge. After national service he joined the staff of the Oxford University Agricultural Economics Research Institute in 1959 as a research assistant, and was appointed to a University Lectureship in Agricultural Economics in 1964. In 1967 he took up an appointment in the Department of Economics in the University of Liverpool, and was appointed Brunner Professor of Economic Science in 1970. He has written for the *Journal of Agricultural Economics, Farm Economist, Economic Journal, Journal of the Royal Statistical Society, Westminster Bank Review, Town and Country Planning, Town Planning Review*, and the *Estates Gazette*.

Acknowledgements

I should like to acknowledge the help of my former colleagues at the Agricultural Economics Institute, Oxford University, Mr Colin Clark and Dr D. Wood, who read a large part of the First Edition of this *Paper*. The later versions have been improved as a result of many discussions with Mr J. S. Dodgson of the University of Liverpool. I am also grateful to the staff of the IEA, particularly Arthur Seldon and Michael Solly, for their continued advice and assistance.

July 1973   G.H.P.

I Setting the Scene

In Britain government action pervades many aspects of economic life. The sharpest manifestation is seen in the extent to which the use of the nation's resources falls directly under the influence of centralised decision-making. On current account, excluding transfer payments, the central government and local authorities spend, respectively, 12·7 and 8·5 per cent of gross national product, while their capital expenditure accounts for a further 5·5 per cent. If public corporations are added the latter figure rises to 9·3 per cent of GNP, representing some 45 per cent of total gross capital formation in the economy.

The magnitude of these figures does not tell the whole story, for the private sector is critically affected by the way public funds are spent. This is most obvious when one considers the influence of government on the location of industry and other economic activities. By providing roads, rail services and power supplies, through expenditure on new towns and town expansions, together with legislative provisions embodied in the wide range of planning regulations, government action exerts a vast influence on the shape of the economy.

Government decision-making: criteria of allocation

Attempts must therefore be made to investigate methods of analysis which facilitate and rationalise government decision-making. The central problem is that of 'priorities', a short-hand term for the criteria of allocating resources between competing uses in the absence of markets. Confident claims are constantly being made about the desirability of this or that government action, but it is evident that a large part of public spending is voted on the basis of hunch, guesswork, horse trading or barely concealed electoral calculations. In the words of a *Times* special correspondent, written during the period in the mid-1960's when there was considerable debate surrounding the question of government expenditure:

'The truth is that many major public expenditure decisions have been taken since the war by old-fashioned "muddle through", "rule of thumb" methods. Investment has been pitifully neglected in some cases while in other spheres public money has been lavished often with a very hazy idea of the return to be expected'.[1]

A few examples of the choices will suffice to convey an impression of the almost baffling difficulty of the decisions that must be made. How are we to weigh road

[1] 'More Rigorous Appraisal for Public Spending', *The Times*, 26 January, 1965.

11

investment against the demands of state education and the National Health Service? How much should be spent on reshaping our towns and cities? Should more new towns be built? Should we attempt to save the best agricultural land at the cost of more expensive building on poorer sites or by building high blocks of flats? What should be spent on industrial research facilities and in which industries? How should public corporations make investment decisions? And how should the returns from funds in 'public' projects compare, not only with one another, but also with the advantages of allowing finance to find its way into private industry through the mechanism of the capital market by which funds are attracted to the points of highest profitability? In short, what information should be included in calculations of costs and benefits assessing the economic viability of public investment programmes?

Not surprisingly any method which promises to bring calculated precision to the aid of centralised allocation is hailed as a major 'breakthrough' in economic planning techniques. It is for this reason that the past decade has witnessed a growth of interest in what are termed cost-benefit appraisals. Indeed the phrase 'cost-benefit' (or 'social cost-benefit') has to some extent become a 'gimmick' expression. It has an air of mystery surrounding it like 'input-output', 'linear programming', 'discounted cash flow', 'critical path analysis' and other developing quantitative methods. According to *The Times*,[1] cost-benefit analysis has been 'catching on' while the *Guardian*[2] described it as 'currently the most fashionable branch of economics'. In the same vein Professor B. R. Williams,[3] at the 1964 meeting of the British Association for the Advancement of Science, called for proper studies to be made of the relative costs and benefits obtained from social activity. He argued that since resources cannot be stretched to do all the things that we would like:

> 'there is continuing need to discover and explain the costs and benefits of different lines of action, and to see that our social control systems help resources to flow into the appropriate channels'.

Since the Treasury too, prompted by the 1961 Plowden Report, became more interested in sharpening methods of controlling and appraising expenditure, cost-benefit techniques have attracted growing attention in Whitehall.

Pioneer studies in US and UK

Though the underlying concepts have been familiar to economists for over 50 years, the pioneering empirical work was, as so often, undertaken in the USA in the 1950s on the large-scale development of major river valleys.[4] Another early application was

---

[1] *Ibid.*
[2] 'A Place for Hunch and Analysis', *Guardian*, 28 August, 1964.
[3] 'Economics in Unwonted Places', *Economic Journal*, March 1965, pp. 20-30.
[4] For example, J. V. Krutilla and Otto Eckstein, *Multiple Purpose River Development*, Johns Hopkins University Press, 1958.

in traffic studies in the state of Oregon (1937).[1] Interest in the subject in Britain developed from Professor G. P. Wibberley's studies of land allocation between agriculture and urban development (1959),[2] from the inquiry by Mr C. D. Foster and Professor M. E. Beesley into the economics of the construction of the Victoria Line extension to the London underground network (1963),[3] and from the Road Research Laboratory's appraisal of the economics of the M1 (1960).[4] Urban planners became familiar with the technique through Dr Nathaniel Lichfield's[5] pioneering (1956) of a 'planning balance sheet' approach to the analysis of urban development and from the Buchanan Report on Traffic in Towns (1963).[6]

Apart from Professor Williams' advocacy, a particularly extreme view of the potentiality of cost-benefit studies was exemplified by Professor Peter Hall's statement in *Labour's New Frontiers*:[7]

'We have begun to grope our way towards a practical concept of economic planning which may prove, in a few years' time, to be as revolutionary in its policy implications as was the Keynesian revolution in economics thirty years ago. It also originated, many years ago, with a Cambridge economist: Keynes's contemporary Pigou. It is the concept of social costs and benefits. Pigou pointed out that in a capitalist society, individual entrepreneurs consider only the items that feature in their own balance sheets. There are, however, others which society must reckon with, though the entrepreneur does not. If a factory owner's chimneys pollute the air, that is a social cost. If he builds a beautiful house for himself, and that improves the view, that is a social benefit. In both cases society is not responsible, but it feels the effect. This leads to the revolutionary concept that we can actually add up the social costs and benefits, in money terms, by asking what value people would themselves put on them. We can then express them as a rate of return on capital, as an ordinary capitalist would, and so determine our investment rationally, from the point of view of the community as a whole, just as the capitalist can now do from his private point of view.'

In subsequent paragraphs Professor Hall made it clear that he regarded the technique as one of the keys to 'economic advance' which should be applied as a means of checking investment programmes including 'our broad strategy of regional development and the detailed planning of our cities'.

[1] C. B. McCullough and J. Beakey, 'The Economics of Highway Planning', *Technical Bulletin* 7, Oregon State Highway Commission, 1937.
[2] *Agriculture and Urban Growth*, Michael Joseph, 1959.
[3] 'Estimating the social benefit of constructing an underground railway in London', *Journal of the Royal Statistical Society*, Vol. 126, Part I, 1963.
[4] T. M. Coburn, M. E. Beesley and D. J. Reynolds, *The London-Birmingham Motor Way— Traffic and Economics*, Road Research Laboratory Technical Paper No. 46, HMSO, 1960.
[5] Nathaniel Lichfield, *Economics of Planned Development*, Estates Gazette, 1956.
[6] *Traffic in Towns*, HMSO, 1963.
[7] André Deutsch, 1964, p. 173.

Caution and scepticism on value of cost-benefit analysis

A position has now been reached (1973) in which many examples of the use of cost-benefit analysis techniques can be quoted. Apart from studies of water resource development, road and rail investment and land-use analysis, the following pages discuss work on education, health, recreation, ports and airports, housing, research and development, and regional planning. Growth in the volume of literature, however, must not be regarded as a sign of general approbation. The technique has its critics. Mr John Brunner,[1] for example, after surveying the parlous state of welfare economics,[2] described cost-benefit analysis as a 'phoenix' arising from the wreckage which attempts in a not very convincing manner to set monetary values on goods and services for which no market exists. In a similarly strong vein Professor Peter Self[3] dismissed the efforts of the Roskill Commission[4] to apply cost-benefit methods to the choice of a site for the third London Airport as 'nonsense on stilts'. In a long academic article reviewing the main versions of the concept, Professor A. R. Prest and Mr Ralph Turvey reached a more qualified view than that of the enthusiasts.[5]

The object of this *Paper* is to look more closely into the origin of the concept, provide examples of its practical application, and outline some of the difficulties associated with it. Developments of the technique have raised many problems of principle and practice and it is probably too early to decide whether cost-benefit appraisals are likely to be a godsend or to forecast that disillusion will set in. The main aim is to provide information without being either destructively critical or unduly optimistic.

---

[1] 'The New Idolatry' in Arthur Seldon (ed.), *Rebirth of Britain*, Pan Books, 1964.
[2] 'Theoretical welfare economics is that branch of study which endeavours to formulate propositions by which we may rank, on the scale of better or worse, alternative economic situations open to society'. (E. J. Mishan, 'A Survey of Welfare Economics, 1939-59', *Economic Journal*, June 1960.) Welfare economists have attempted to state criteria for increasing social welfare and the conditions for an 'optimum' situation (where no one can be made better off without making someone else worse off). Broadly speaking they have therefore been concerned with the efficient allocation of resources.
[3] ' "Nonsense on Stilts": Cost Benefit Analysis and the Roskill Commission', *Political Quarterly*, Vol. 41, 1970.
[4] Commission on the Third London Airport, *Report*, HMSO, 1971. For further discussion of the Roskill Report, below, pp. 49-56.
[5] 'Cost Benefit Analysis: A Survey', *Economic Journal*, December 1965.

14

II Some Fundamental Concepts

The term 'cost-benefit' analysis is sometimes prefaced by the word 'social'. Professor Hall, in the above quotation, refers to the distinction between private and social costs and benefits and to the rate of return on capital as a means of rational decision-making. 'Cost-effectiveness' is used to describe a variant of the basic cost-benefit technique. Anyone who reads economic literature soon senses that such jargon can easily become the source of confusion unless its meaning is clear and consistent. A useful start can be made by clarifying the word 'appraisal' as it is used in economics. What steps are needed before expenditure on building a road or a factory, or on providing a service, is economically worthwhile?

Economic appraisal

Briefly, the usual method for testing the 'soundness' of proposed activities requires a calculation of the value of the resources to be employed in them (the costs) which are compared with the value of the goods or services to be produced (the benefits). In appraising an investment it is the normal practice to subtract from the annual value of receipts all variable or running costs, leaving a residual which can be expressed as an annual rate of return on the capital employed. If the anticipated returns compare favourably with the prospective rates obtainable from alternative uses to which the capital might be put, the proposed project may be regarded as 'sound', from the point of view of a private business. The rate of return must also exceed the cost of obtaining capital as expressed through the rate of interest.

In a competitive market economy, and indeed this is its object, the value of benefits yielded by an activity is reflected through the workings of the price mechanism in the amounts which ultimate consumers are prepared to pay for goods and services. Similarly the costs which have to be met are reflected through markets for the factors of production—labour, capital, land, entrepreneurial talents. In the last analysis these costs must be related to consumers' valuations of the goods which would have become available through using resources in other ways. They are 'opportunity costs', or the measure of the value of alternative lines of activity. If the returns on capital in one use, after allowing for the degree of risk associated with it, are higher than those in other uses, the forces of competition will tend to bring about transfers of resources from areas of low to areas of higher return unless this movement is frustrated by lack of information or other influences. That returns may be different is a reflection of consumers' preferences, improvements in technique and the development of knowledge; and reallocation as a result of changes in any of them represents a useful social function.

The determination of rates of return on capital, which acts as one of the prime movers in the allocation of resources in the private sector of the economy, can itself be regarded as an application of cost-benefit analysis. In his British Association paper Professor Williams was correct in emphasising that the technique is an integral part of economic life. Though he questioned whether businessmen pay sufficient attention to the refinement of their methods of investment appraisal—or indeed whether in many cases anything other than the most rudimentary calculations are performed— his discussion of cost-benefit analysis in the private sector showed that the concept is intrinsically not new.[1]

The government sector

This picture of a market economy is idealised, especially in failing to point out that rates of return on capital which determine resource allocation within it may be distorted by excessive monopoly influences and other restrictive practices so that the price mechanism fails to reflect basic preferences. Nonetheless the prices of outputs serve as approximate guide-lines. By contrast a whole range of public services are supplied *without direct prices being charged for them*.[2] Apart from the nationalised industries, the organisation and the scale of supply must be decided in the absence of a market-determined indicator of benefits received.

The reasons are numerous. In the first place some types of goods and services must be provided, if at all, through public authorities and paid for by taxation (or, as in education and health services, partly by direct charges). Here we are concerned with 'collective goods' which cater for a 'group want'. A classic example is defence, where the presence of armed forces affords a measure of protection to all citizens. It is hardly conceivable, furthermore, that individuals who became convinced of a need for increasing the supply of armaments would proceed to make purchases 'in the market' and place them at the disposal of the state.[3] Indeed the logical course of action for the individual would be to campaign politically for increased expenditures in the hope that other members of the community would be prepared to sanction

---

[1] Williams, *loc. cit.* In this paper some of the new techniques of appraisal were discussed. A fuller analysis of the techniques in the private sector is in A. J. Merrett and Allen Sykes, *The Finance and Analysis of Capital Projects*, Longmans, 1963, or C. J. Hawkins and D. W. Pearce, *Capital Investment Appraisal*, Macmillan Studies in Economics, Macmillan, 1971. The purist would probably object to applying the term 'cost-benefit analysis' to a purely commercial investment on the ground that 'private' and 'social' returns (below, pp. 17-19) may not coincide. It would seem wise, therefore, not to extend usage of the phrase to commercial investment appraisal.

[2] E.g., roads, schools and health services.

[3] The case is nevertheless arguable: William A. Niskanen, Jr., *Bureaucracy: Servant or Master?*, Hobart Paperback No. 5, IEA, 1973.

additional taxation.[1] In short, when public goods are involved, ordinary market forces may be incapable of detecting a demand for them, and of organising supply. Though such group wants may at first sight seem rare, they are common in Western economies. Defence and police services,[2] flood protection, an unpolluted atmosphere, freedom from noise, and the preservation of landscape provide examples.

The existence of group wants provides the fundamental *raison d'être* for public services, although drawing a distinction between collective goods, which cannot be supplied by a free market mechanism, and goods that can, is notoriously difficult. In Britain the central government and local authorities provide a wide range of services as 'public goods', for many of which, notably health and education, there is considerable room for argument whether supply could be more effectively organised through a market,[3] hedged with safeguards to protect standards and the poorer members of the community. In such cases the justification for government intervention can be based only on such grounds as egalitarianism, paternalism, divergences between private and social costs and benefits (below) and, sometimes, the allegedly superior efficiency of the public sector.

Though public goods are supplied in the absence of market indication of benefits received, guidance is not completely lacking. In the last analysis decisions on the quantity and quality supplied rest with the ballot box; the decision-taking process is political.[4] But though this method may to some extent lay down very broad guide-lines it is idle to pretend that it can make individual, detailed decisions capable of reflecting social needs and preferences. In practice these decisions have very largely come to rest with ministers and public officials. It is against this background that interest in cost-benefit analysis has grown. It indicates a search for tools of economic appraisal to assess the wisdom of alternative courses of action for application in areas where a market is not, or cannot be, used.

Private and social costs and benefits

The distinction between private and social costs and benefits was made famous by the late Professor A. C. Pigou at the beginning of the century. In the course of his treatise on welfare economics he argued that there may be circumstances in which

---

[1] This situation gives rise to what Professor J. M. Buchanan has called the problem of the 'free rider', the individual who benefits from a service though he may pay nothing for it. (*The Inconsistencies of the National Health Service*, Occasional Paper 7, IEA, 1965, especially the suggestions for further reading on p. 23.)

[2] In recent years police services have increasingly been supplied in the market, e.g., for protection against theft: R. L. Carter, *Theft in the Market,* Hobart Paper 60, IEA, 1974. Some police and other government services could be supplied in return for direct payment by prices, e.g., charges are, or could be, made for exceptional policing. (Cf. Carter, *ibid.*)

[3] Ralph Harris and Arthur Seldon, *Choice in Welfare 1970*, IEA, 1971, discuss the main issues and attempt to reconstruct a hypothetical market for education and health services.

[4] For a penetrating analysis of the relationship between economic and political choice, T. W. Hutchison, *Markets and the Franchise*, Occasional Paper 10, IEA, 1966.

market forces fail to encompass all costs and all benefits. This failure has been noted for collective goods but it may also apply where there are 'externalities'. In Pigou's words:

'The essence of the matter is that one person A, in the course of rendering some service for which payment is made, to a second person B, incidentally also renders services or disservices to other persons, of such a sort that payment cannot be exacted from the benefited parties or compensation enforced on behalf of the injured parties.'[1]

Social costs may be defined as the sum total of the costs of an economic action.[2] Private costs are those which affect the decisions of its performers. For example, in production undertaken for a market, what are the private costs with which the entrepreneur is concerned? First he must pay labour at least as much as it would be worth in other uses; he must compete for materials, land and capital; he must earn his own rewards. All of these also represent 'opportunity costs' to society at large. They are social costs reflected through the market. Over and above them may be additional 'external' costs not impinging on the entrepreneur, for instance smoke nuisance.[3]

Similar effects may occur on the other side of the equation. Benefits are reflected in the amounts paid by consumers for goods produced; but, in addition, favourable 'externalities' might also accrue to society. A dam, in addition to generating electricity for sale in the market, brings flood protection benefits for which no payment is made. If there are external social costs, the private rate of return on capital, which is what interests the entrepreneur, over-states the social returns; conversely, it may under-estimate the social return if there are external benefits.

External effects can manifest themselves in many ways. We may define a 'production-to-production' linkage as one in which the scale of activity of one production unit affects the output of other units given no change in their 'inputs' of labour, capital or other factors. In mining, pumping water from one shaft may reduce flooding in

[1] A. C. Pigou, *The Economics of Welfare*, 4th edn., Macmillan, 1950, p. 183.

[2] We have here defined 'social' costs to *include* private costs. This is the practice recommended by D. W. Pearce and S. G. Sturmey, 'Private and Social Costs and Benefits: A Note on Terminology', *Economic Journal,* March 1966, and adopted by E. J. Mishan, *The Costs of Economic Growth,* Staples Press, 1967, p. 53. It can be somewhat confusing in that popular terminology frequently appears to use the term 'social cost' to cover only that part of total cost to the community which is *not* reflected in the market. The latter can better be regarded as 'external diseconomies'. A good introduction to the high-level theoretical discussion of the concepts of externality is provided by W. J. Baumol, *Welfare Economics and the Theory of the State*, 2nd edn., London School of Economics and G. Bell & Sons, 1965 (particularly the introduction and pp. 46-8 for bibliography). There are also useful references, and an interesting discussion of spill-over effects between areas resulting from the mutual interaction of local government programmes, in A. Williams, 'The Optimal Provision of Public Goods in a System of Local Government', *Journal of Political Economy,* February 1966.

[3] The market *may* reflect the smoke nuisance, e.g., through the decline of local property values. But the costs of the nuisance would still not be borne by the factory imposing it.

18

other mines and enable their output to be increased. A new dam constructed upstream from existing plant may enhance the control of water flow so increasing downstream electricity generating capacity. A 'production-to-consumption' externality occurs when productive activities affect consumption; smoke nuisance, noise and water pollution are examples. 'Consumption-to-consumption' effects may also occur—for example, playing radios in parks. 'Consumption-to-production' effects are typified by walkers trampling on growing crops.

There is no clear boundary between these categories, but they serve to illustrate the pervading influence of possible beneficial or injurious external consequences which may not be reflected in market prices. The external linkage may be extremely close or widely diffused, often impinging upon the enjoyment of collective goods. Rather more complex examples are those in which activity 'today' precludes other activities in the future: thus urban development may reduce agricultural output. Though cost-price relationships may indicate a collective desire to re-allocate land between these uses, once the process has occurred it cannot be reversed easily.

Policy implications

Since many of the examples of cost-benefit appraisal discussed below have strong Pigovian undertones it is useful, at this stage, to mention some of the implications for economic policy of the distinction between private and social costs and benefits.

Though generally an advocate of the market in allocating resources, Pigou held that modification of its operation may be necessary to ensure that the effects of external social consequences should impinge upon those who create them. His classic recommendation was that modification should be achieved by levying taxes upon people creating unfavourable externalities, and paying subsidies to those creating favourable externalities.

The logic underlying this solution is simple. The creator of unfavourable external effects will choose a scale of operation for his activity which reflects only his private interest (and, if he produces goods or services, the interests of those who, through the market, indicate their preferences to him). The larger the scale of the activity the larger will be the unfavourable side-effects which do not directly impinge upon him. A tax designed to reflect the magnitude of the externality should force the person responsible to reconsider the scale of his activity by adding to his private costs the amount necessary to equate private and social costs. This process may have the result of reducing external consequences; if it does not there is theoretically a fund available from the tax from which to compensate those injured. In this way the marginal costs associated with each scale of activity, which determine the optimum *'private'* scale of operation, become a full reflection of marginal *'social'* costs. The creator of favourable external effects, conversely, would be induced by a subsidy to expand the scale of his activity to an extent which might not be privately profitable

19

in its absence. The tax or subsidy is intended to have the effect of altering the private rates of return on capital employed so that they represent social rates of return.

Who bears external costs?

So much for the theory and the resulting policy proposals. Several comments should be made. In the first place it must not too easily be assumed that external consequences are unreflected in market transactions. It is often held that industry's capacity to create an unfavourable and unhealthy environment represents an infliction of external costs—a 'production-to-consumption' effect. Even here, however, there is room to argue whether the unfavourable environment might reduce the supply of labour to the enterprises and so cause wages, for example, to be higher than they otherwise would be. In this way private costs to entrepreneurs are raised, and labour is to some extent compensated for living in unpleasant conditions. Hence the 'London allowance'—formal in some public employments, informal but common in private employments. While it would be unwise to assert firmly that such externalities are always reflected in market costs and prices, it would be equally rash to hold the opposite view. In 'production-to-production' externalities, e.g., mine-shafts, the effects can be reciprocal, so that the parties concerned have every incentive to bargain together and possibly to merge.[1]

Secondly, as will be apparent later, there are clearly stubborn practical difficulties in identifying and valuing external effects. Many are therefore dealt with by regulation.[2] Examples are most numerous in town and country planning, but are also encountered in air and river pollution, noise abatement and parking restrictions. In such ways obvious social costs resulting from private actions are made to impinge directly on the individuals creating them.

[1] Controversy relating to market modification has a long history: F. H. Knight, 'Some Fallacies in the Interpretation of Social Cost', *Quarterly Journal of Economics*, June 1924, pp. 182-206; R. H. Coase, 'The Problem of Social Cost,' *Journal of Law and Economics*, October 1960; J. M. Buchanan and W. C. Stubblebine, 'Externality', *Economica*, November 1962; Ralph Turvey, 'On Divergence between Social Cost and Private Cost', *ibid.*, August 1963; A. R. Prest and Ralph Turvey, 'Cost Benefit Analysis: A Survey', *Economic Journal*, December 1965. There is also an extremely clear discussion of a whole range of issues in E. J. Mishan, *The Costs of Economic Growth*, Staples Press, 1967. In addition to his polemical attack on the current obsession with growth at all costs, Dr Mishan urges the need to find methods whereby those responsible for external diseconomies can be made to bear the costs of their actions *via* new, market-based methods of pricing. One of his main arguments is that more explicit formal recognition should be given to amenity rights such as privacy, quiet and clean air which are not often treated as falling firmly within the framework of discussion and analysis. If actions could be pursued against violators of such rights, he holds, there would be clear incentives for creators of external diseconomies to attempt voluntary agreement with those affected. Mutually acceptable solutions could be reached by bargaining. Failing this solution he suggests separate and inviolate facilities for people who wish to opt out of a system in which external diseconomies (noise, fumes, traffic congestion and air pollution) are rampant and increasingly obvious. An opposing view is that of Professor Wilfred Beckerman, 'Why we need economic growth', *Lloyds Bank Review*, October 1971.

[2] The limitations of regulation are discussed by Neil H. Jacoby and F. G. Pennance in *The Polluters: Industry or Government?*, Occasional Paper 36, IEA, 1971.

Proposals for road pricing in the form of extra charges placed on drivers to reflect the social costs of traffic congestion are essentially an example of Pigovian market modification.[1] The argument here is that the individual driver absorbs private costs in the form of delay to himself but does not take into account the delay he inflicts on others (an external cost). The state of the work in traffic engineering is such that it has advanced to the point at which the physical effects can be quantified.[2] On similar lines it has been argued elsewhere that industrial or commercial activities undertaken in large conurbations, though deterred to some extent by higher wage levels, could be further reduced by payroll taxes.[3] The spreading conurbations might also be contained by ensuring that commuters are not encouraged by artificially low public transport charges, and the road situation improved by more sharply rising charges on heavy vehicles that cause congestion.[4] Interesting proposals have recently been advanced by Professors Lord Zuckerman and Wilfred Beckerman[5] for charges, on a rising scale of severity, on local authorities responsible for the discharge of untreated sewage into coastal waters.

These examples of market-modifying measures should be seen as the application of 'marginal social cost charging' criteria as developed from the Pigovian analysis. The important point in the development of the cost-benefit appraisals described later is that the economist may be faced with taking into account not only the direct but also the indirect consequences of a particular investment. In short, in cost-benefit analysis of public investment schemes he may be faced not only with problems associated with collective goods, but might additionally wish to appraise some of the possible external effects.

[1] G. J. Roth, *A Self-financing Road System,* Research Monograph 3, IEA, 1966.
[2] The Smeed Report, *Road Pricing: The Economic and Technical Possibilities,* HMSO, 1964, and G. J. Roth, *Paying for Parking,* Hobart Paper 33, IEA, 1965, App. 3.
[3] Colin Clark and G. H. Peters, 'Location Taxes for Industry', *Town and Country Planning,* March 1964. It should be noted that in this article there are no concrete estimates of the true social costs of urban growth. The design of an optimal system of payroll taxation would require these costs to be measured.
[4] For other suggestions, B. R. Williams, *loc. cit.,* p. 27. One example quoted concerns favourable tax treatment of research and training expenditure in private industry on the ground that it generates a social benefit.
[5] Minority Report in *Royal Commission on Environmental Pollution: Third Report,* HMSO, September 1972.

III Some Major Applications of Cost-Benefit Analysis

Cost-benefit analyses normally comprise several stages. First, the project must be defined and a list made of the current benefits and costs to be included. This may appear to state the obvious, but in practice it raises a number of fundamental issues. As benefits one must include those goods and services produced for sale in the market or accruing as collective goods: current operating costs associated with the project must be subtracted. But how far is the economist to go in evaluating external benefits and costs? Some members of society may be much affected by them, others may feel only a slight backwash. In short, who is to constitute the 'society' which the appraisal is to cover? This problem must be kept in mind throughout the discussion.

Secondly, the list of benefits and costs, direct or indirect, must be reduced to monetary values in order to arrive at an estimate of the current net benefit of the project (if any). Difficulties arise not only in placing a monetary value on collective or other goods or services, but also appear if the scale of the project is so large as to have marked effects on the prevailing market prices.[1] This is the problem of 'indivisibility'. If these difficulties have been faced, the analyst is left with an estimate of annual net benefit of the project.

Thirdly, the final step is to compare the stream of annual net benefits with the capital cost of the project. In its simplest terms the annual value, after an allowance has been made for depreciation of capital assets, might be expressed as a percentage rate of return on the investment: the problem of appraisal is then to consider whether this rate of return is high enough to justify proceeding with the project. In other words, is the value of capital in this use at least equal to the price of capital as represented by the rate of interest? At this stage of the analysis two sets of problems have to be faced. The first is mechanical: the exact form of the investment appraisal method to be used. The second is fundamental: choosing a rate of interest (or discount) to act as a critical 'cut-off' rate within the calculation.

Methods of appraisal

The mechanical difficulties may be summarised thus: if cost-benefit analysis is an appropriate method for choosing between similar but mutually exclusive investments

---

[1] '. . . cost-benefit techniques as so far developed are least relevant and serviceable for what one might call large-size investment decisions. If investment decisions are so large relatively to a given economy (e.g. a major dam project in a small country) that they are likely to alter the constellation of relative outputs and prices over the whole economy, the standard technique is likely to fail us, for nothing less than some sort of general equilibrium approach would suffice in such cases.' (A. R. Prest and Ralph Turvey, *op. cit.*, p. 685.)

(e.g. a large or small dam, a two- or three-lane road) where benefits have been evaluated in monetary terms, difficulty can nonetheless arise in ranking the projects in order of preference and in choosing between them.

Three procedures can be used. First, in the net present-value method a discount rate is chosen and is used to convert a time-stream of net benefits (i.e., benefits minus running costs) to present-value terms. Investment costs are then deducted and the projects appraised in the light of the resulting net present values. Secondly, the implicit rate of return on capital employed yielded by each project may be found by mathematical methods. The resulting 'internal rates of return' can then be used in the appraisal process to identify the project where the rate is highest. Thirdly, the present values of the benefit stream can be expressed as 'benefit-cost' ratios with the denominator representing investment charges. Choice of project here would depend on the size of the resulting ratios. Unfortunately these methods do not necessarily point to the same project as being optimal—the order may change with differing appraisal techniques. There is now a fairly general agreement that the net present-value method is preferable to the other two, though Dr Mishan has recently shown that a number of difficulties remain.[1]

Though it is often confusing to the reader of cost-benefit studies to find alternative methods in use within the appraisal calculations, the difficulties outlined above are basically practical rather than conceptual. But in the choice of the 'cut-off' rate of interest, or of discount, formidable questions of principle arise immediately.

Choice of 'cut-off' rate

First, a function of the rate of interest is to allocate capital funds between alternative uses. Economic theory suggests that the 'equi-marginal principle' should come into play and that the return on capital in one use should be equated with that in competing uses. In short, the 'cut-off' rate for the appraisal of a project needs to reflect the 'opportunity cost' of capital. For three reasons it is by no means easy to say precisely what this is by reference to any one rate established in the capital market:

[1] E. J. Mishan, *Cost-Benefit Analysis*, Allen and Unwin, 1971, especially Part IV. Appraisal techniques are explained in the texts cited above (p. 16, footnote 1) and a good summary is provided by Martin Wohl and Brian V. Martin, 'Evaluating Road Projects', *Journal of Transport Economics and Policy*, January 1967. Basically the major difficulty (in what can be a rather complex problem) is associated with the varying scale of possible projects. In the net present-value method the 'cut-off' rate of discount is applied to the benefit stream and, for any project to be judged viable, the resulting present values must be higher than investment costs. If this is so the internal rate of return would exceed the cut-off rate. For mutually exclusive investments, however, other projects (typically those of smaller scale) could yield higher internal rates of return. A small project with a higher internal rate of return should not be regarded as superior to a larger project if its net present value is lower. Quite simply the investment in scale is economically justified since the 'cut-off' criterion is satisfied. In a similar way the project with the highest ratio of benefit to cost need not be the one which maximises net present value. For this reason benefit-cost ratios are often calculated in incremental terms (below, p. 27, for an example).

(i) A government agency supplying a service and competing for capital funds against private enterprise demands may have access to capital obtained through an issue of government securities which, since the issue is underwritten by the government and risk-free, may be obtained on more favourable terms than an issue by a private organisation. The agency project has the cards stacked in its favour especially if it is capital-intensive (i.e. using more capital than labour compared with other industries) with a long life. This objection has been recognised for the nationalised industries where a 'trial rate of discount', designed to reflect the opportunity cost of capital, is now applied.[1]

(ii) Even if this procedure is acceptable, it is still not easy to determine the relevant 'opportunity cost'. The yields on the securities issued by private enterprises (apart from being notoriously variable because of differing degrees of risk) are arrived at after company taxes have been paid. Hence the underlying rates of return on capital employed tend to be higher than any set of returns reflected in the market.[2]

(iii) Many government projects are undertaken with finance which may, in part at least, be raised from taxation. How can the true 'opportunity cost' of capital be gauged when it is not raised in the market in competition with bids for other uses?

Private and social time preferences

The second question of principle shifts the whole argument to an entirely different level. Market-determined interest rates also, to some degree, reflect society's preferences between present and future consumption. These preferences in part limit the total fund available for investment in *particular periods*. Is there a distinction between the time preferences of private individuals, which in the last analysis must be related to the length of human life, and that of society as a whole, which must at least be regarded as somewhat longer? In short, the use of capital to strengthen the framework of society for the future might be allowable even though the annual returns are low (the reclamation or conservation of land is a good example). The school of thought that subscribes to this view argues that *private* rates of time preference may be 'too high' and that a case can be made for using a lower 'social' rate of time preference in many cost-benefit applications.

[1] White Paper, *Economic and Financial Obligations of the Nationalised Industries*, Cmnd. 3477, HMSO, November 1967. For a discussion of returns obtained, G. Polanyi, *Comparative Returns from Investment in Nationalised Industries*, Background Memorandum 1, IEA, 1968, which doubts the value of cost-benefit analysis.

[2] This difficulty arose in discussion of the nationalised industry trial rate of discount which was originally fixed at 8 per cent. A. M. Alfred, 'The Correct Yardstick for State Investment', *District Bank Review*, June 1968, argued that the rate was somewhat low and should be raised to 10-11 per cent.

Difficulties of this nature are common in cost-benefit studies, and will arise constantly in the examples quoted below.[1] Indeed, it is now widely held that choice of an appropriate rate is purely a value-judgement, and that it is impossible to lay down any clear-cut rules of procedure. But if this is so, does it not reduce the whole process from an exact science to an 'art' dependent on personal judgement, preferences and perhaps prejudice?

United States water resource development studies

The *vade mecum* for much subsequent work in cost-benefit analysis is found in the various studies of water resource development in the United States.[2] Though at first sight the questions which arise may seem remote to a British audience, some recent proposals, such as those for damming Morecambe Bay, the Solway Firth and the Wash, give rise to similar appraisal problems.

USA water resource development projects have been designed for several purposes. Typically, building a dam will yield a hydro-electricity potential on site; storage facilities may be a source of irrigation potential; flood control and navigational benefits may result; and if the new dam is upstream from existing structures it may improve their generating capacity. The construction of dams may be undertaken by the Federal or State government, or by private enterprises (normally power companies) operating under licence. Three important valuation problems may emerge:

1. A value has to be placed on the electricity generated at site. The difficulty here is that the increment in power supply, because of the 'lumpiness' of the investment, may be large enough to depress the market price.

2. Because the new structures may influence downstream generating capacity a direct 'production-to-production' externality may result. There are similar difficulties where the potential irrigation capacity is likely to be enhanced.

[1] Readers interested in exhaustive analyses of the role of interest and discount rates may consult: M. S. Feldstein, 'The Social Time Preference Discount Rate in Cost Benefit Analysis', *Economic Journal*, June 1964; R. Turvey, 'Present Value Versus Internal Rate of Return', *Economic Journal*, March 1963; M. S. Feldstein and J. S. Flemming, 'The Problem of Time Stream Evaluation: Present Value Versus Internal Rate of Return', *Bulletin of Oxford University Institute of Statistics*, February 1964; M. S. Feldstein, 'Net Social Benefit Calculations and the Public Investment Decision', *Oxford Economic Papers*, March 1964. A summary is provided by E. J. Mishan, *Cost-Benefit Analysis, op. cit.*

[2] Major works include Krutilla and Eckstein, *loc. cit.*; Otto Eckstein, *Water Resource Development*, Harvard University Press, Cambridge, Mass., 1961; Arthur Maas *et al., Design of Water Resource Systems*, Macmillan, New York, 1962; Julius Hirschleifer *et al., Water Supply: Economics, Technology and Policy*, Cambridge University Press, 1961; J. V. Krutilla, *The Columbia River Treaty: The Economics of an International River Basin Development*, J. S. Bain, R. E. Caves and J. Margolis, *Northern California's Water Industry*, and Allen V. Kneese and S. C. Smith (eds.), *Water Research and Economic Analysis* (all published by Johns Hopkins University Press, Baltimore, for Resources for the Future). Some discussion of British conditions is given by J. J. Warford in 'Water Requirements —the Investment Decision in the Water Supply Industry', *Manchester School*, January 1966.

25

3. Externalities, whether social benefits or costs, may also affect 'group wants'. Flood protection is the classic example.

In this process gains are normally compared with costs to arrive at a figure of 'net benefits'. But there are further difficulties. Engineering possibilities may be such that a stretch of river could be developed in a number of ways or the scale of the project altered. Thus it is not simply a question of appraising the economic benefits of a single project but of comparing alternative projects with one another. All net benefits and annual operating costs, together with capital costs, must be considered.

It is important also to specify the nature of the items the analyst chooses to measure. If investments were being appraised from the purely 'private' or commercial viewpoint the dominating features would be the value of electricity generated, the capital costs of borrowing in the market, and annual running costs. In short, the externality effects would be ignored. In view of the considerable 'production-to-production' externality in generating capacity, legal arrangements could be made to require operators of down-stream stations to contribute to costs. But the difficulty remains of ensuring that all beneficial externalities are taken into account in a private investment appraisal. Similarly an appraisal made by a government agency might have to stop short at some point. To take an example, extra generating capacity could be a potent factor affecting the distribution of industry. The benefits to industrialists would theoretically be reflected in the price they were prepared to pay for power, but costs or benefits would also probably accrue to other people. Though in river development the range of costs and benefits included focuses fairly clearly on the effects on uses of water alone, even the most wide-ranging appraisal must have its boundaries. This problem will be met again.

There can also be another fundamental difference in valuation procedure between a private and a social appraisal. To a company, the important magnitude is additional revenue; the price used in valuation is therefore that at which extra power would sell. To consumers, on the other hand, price represents the valuation they place on additional (marginal) units of a commodity. Thus total revenue may fall far short of reflecting the value of the large, rather than marginal, increment in supply which might become available. It is often suggested that value should be approximated by using a 'shadow' price half way between the existing and the new price.[1] This difficulty also arises in valuing downstream increments in generating capacity.

The valuation of benefits for which no charge is made is not as difficult as it might seem. Flood control benefits might, for example, be valued in one of two ways. If the incidence of floods can be determined and the amount of damage assessed, there is some guide to the benefit conferred by a project which makes floods less likely. Alternatively, valuation might be made by analysing insurance records to determine the amounts people are paying to minimise their risks. For irrigation water, often

[1] Krutilla and Eckstein, *op. cit.*, p. 74.

not charged for, the task is to value the resulting increment in agricultural output but deducting the estimated value of other resources drawn into agricultural production (to avoid double counting). Similarly navigation benefits might be assessed by estimating cost savings accompanying general development of the river system.

Final appraisal: valuing capital

In the final appraisal there is again the difficulty of capital costs and their annual value. Agencies of the US Government have conventions: the Bureau of the Budget recommends the rate on government securities with terms of maturity as close as possible to the estimated economically useful life of the project. Drs Krutilla and Eckstein have argued that such a practice is hardly defensible where capital is̄ raised through taxation, and have carried out studies based on estimates of the 'social cost' of Federal finance.[1]

Given measured net benefits and annual costs obtained by applying a rate of interest to the capital cost,[2] conventional US practice then focusses attention on incremental benefit-cost ratios. This procedure has the advantage of being useful where a valley might be developed in mutually exclusive ways, for each of which benefits and costs have been estimated. On the basis of the least costly project for which benefits exceed costs the alternatives are worked through stage by stage, additional benefits being set against additional costs. Scale is then expanded to the point where additional benefits are brought as nearly as possible into equality with additional costs.[3] Hence the rule for maximising returns or net benefits, equating marginal cost with marginal gain, is satisfied.

Some of the problems here are essentially Pigovian. If development is undertaken by a private firm whose primary object is typically the generation of power for sale in a market, the scale of development chosen might not be that which maximises 'social net product'. Since private companies under US law are unable to recoup the value of uncompensated benefits, the scale of operation chosen by private profit maximisation might be *less* than desirable if all external repercussions are taken into account. In these circumstances development by a government agency based on social considerations would result in extra costs being incurred. These additional costs can be regarded as a form of Pigovian subsidy.

[1] Krutilla and Eckstein, *op. cit.,* Ch. IV. Briefly this method consists of tracing tax receipts to their source (e.g. persons or companies), and studying the rates of interest and rates of return on personal savings or company investments. The opportunity cost is arrived at by weighting these rates by the proportion of taxation collected from each group.

[2] It will be recalled from the earlier discussion of appraisal methods (p. 23) that a benefit-cost ratio can be formed by discounting benefits to present-value terms, with capital costs forming the denominator. In Krutilla and Eckstein's work one finds that the ratio is obtained from the *annual* value of the benefit stream, with the denominatoɪ being taken as the *annual* cost of capital (including interest and amortisation). The principle is similar.

[3] Eckstein, *op. cit.,* especially Chs. III and IV, discusses the correspondence between assessments based on benefit-cost ratios and rates of return.

It is, of course, no accident that so much work in the US has focussed on the economics of multi-purpose schemes. The externalities are enormous; for example, some large dams are responsible for downstream increments in generating capacity three times the site capacity. Such projects are heavy users of capital and exhibit strong elements of natural monopoly, which have long attracted the attention of governments and economists. It should not be assumed, however, that the calculations can pretend to precise accuracy. Engineering estimates themselves are subject to uncertainty; and valuation at all stages is hazardous. Even in the most promising and most developed application of cost-benefit analysis, conflicts in the choice of scale of development arise from variation in interest rates used in the appraisal process.[1]

Though substantial problems remain, systematic evaluation is thought necessary both because of the large sums appropriated to resource development and as a means of offsetting excessive claims to the expected benefits submitted by those most likely to be affected. Formal analysis of the problems is at least a better guide than the inspired hunch of the politician or public official.

British transport studies

Two of the earlier and most important cost-benefit studies carried out in Britain were on the London-Birmingham motorway (M1) and the Victoria Line extension to the London underground network.

(*a*) *The M1 study.* The motorway study, by a team drawn from the Road Research Laboratory and the University of Birmingham, was largely experimental. The object was partly to test the procedures for estimating the degree of utilisation of new road facilities, with economic assessment as a complementary objective. A decision to proceed with the motorway was taken before the results of the exercise were known.

In terms of cost-benefit methodology the problem posed by roads is that of estimating net benefits where no direct charge is made. The taxes paid by road users cannot in any sense be regarded as a payment; they are more akin to any other form of indirect taxation. The report stated as an objective for economic assessment that:

'In order for the construction of the motorway to be worthwhile it must be shown that the rate of return obtainable is greater than the current rate of interest and (more rigorously) greater than the rates of return obtainable in other uses of capital (including other road improvements).'[2]

How can the returns be measured if no direct price is charged?

[1] Krutilla and Eckstein, *op. cit.*, p. 159. From their case studies instances are available of development in which there would be no conflict between the choice of scale of projects where choice was based on private or social appraisal. (*Ibid.*, p. 196.)
[2] T. M. Coburn, M. E. Beesley and D. J. Reynolds, *The London-Birmingham Motorway, Traffic and Economics,* Road Research Laboratory Technical Paper No. 46, HMSO, 1960, p. 63. For a more accessible account, C. D. Foster, *The Transport Problem,* Blackie, 1963, especially Ch. 11.

The list of benefits in the study included such items as savings in working time by traffic transferring to the motorway, in vehicle time (which could result in road fleets being smaller), in fuel consumption, tyre, brake and clutch wear, in costs of accidents and economies in non-working time. There was one externality: the savings to persons who would continue to use existing roads. A trend factor to reflect the savings likely as a result of the natural growth of traffic was added. The list included benefits only to users of roads. Valuation was undertaken purely from the consumers' point of view. There was no question of attempting to include any far-reaching external effects of the motorway on, for example, the economies of the towns most affected by it. Nor did the study group discuss whether the improved transport network would give a further twist to the spiral of increasing concentration of population in London and the Midlands, which is sometimes held to be detrimental to the development of the economy in general. This question is probably unanswerable by speculation and analysis, of the cost-benefit or any other kind. Indeed at this juncture it is worth remarking on a judgement of Mr C. D. Foster who held that a full social cost-benefit study—in which *all* costs and benefits are included—is by its very nature an impossible practical ideal at which to aim.[1] The line must be drawn somewhere; and in transport studies to date it has been drawn to include only the benefits to users of transport facilities. Indeed Mr Foster described full 'social appraisals' in which all costs and all benefits to whomsoever they may accrue are estimated as a 'piece of utopianism'. The users of transport facilities can be identified, but inclusion of the effects on indirect beneficiaries, or parties injured, is virtually impossible.

Valuing physical magnitudes

What of the physical evaluation of the motorway's effects? A whole range of traffic engineering techniques was employed to estimate the extent to which traffic might be expected to switch to the motorway; likely average speeds were assessed and compared with those on existing roads; petrol consumption was estimated; origin-destination and purpose-of-journey surveys were put in hand, and comparisons made with Continental and American experience.

Difficulties in economic assessment had then to be faced. Here a money value clearly had to be imputed to each of the physical magnitudes estimated. For work-time savings a ready standard of valuation was available—the hourly rates of pay of drivers and passengers. Even here there was the problem of placing a value on time savings by, for example, sales representatives or executives not paid for driving as such. This is a critical weakness since time saving accounted for a large share of annual benefits.[2]

[1] *Ibid.*, pp. 62-65.
[2] For three assumptions relating to speeds total vehicle-cost savings were £749,000, £890,000, £964,000. Working-time savings amounted to £453,000, £624,000 and £766,000 respectively. Savings from reduction in accidents and estimates of the cost of maintenance were £215,000 and £200,000 in each case giving net benefits of £764,000, £905,000 and £979,000.

Another major task was to estimate the extent to which the vehicle fleets of operators habitually using a London-to-Birmingham route might be reduced. As a sample, records supplied by British Road Services were consulted to estimate the physical magnitudes, an economic value being placed upon the resultant figure by using the depreciated capital value of older vehicles in the fleet. The valuation of accident reduction was based on estimates of damage to property and the costs of medical services.

Two further problems remained. First, time savings accrue not only to people travelling in working time. Can additional leisure time be included in the calculation? How is leisure to be valued? To overcome the difficulties, alternative values (10p, 20p, 30p and 40p per hour) were chosen somewhat arbitrarily and the implications for the rate of return explored. The second additional difficulty was connected with the traffic generated by the motorway. Some traffic simply switches to a new road; other journeys not previously undertaken or undertaken other than by road are generated. Calculations based on overseas experience[1] suggested that the order of magnitude might be as high as 31 per cent of the volume of diverted traffic. Benefits would be felt by generated traffic though they could hardly be valued as highly as those to traffic which found it advantageous to travel by road in the less favourable pre-motorway age. So the unit value of benefit to generated traffic was placed at 50 per cent of the unit value to diverting traffic.

In the final appraisal, given a cost of construction of £23·3 million, the crude rate of return when benefits to diverting traffic alone were considered ranged, with varying speed assumptions, from 3·3 to 4·2 per cent. Adding benefits to generated traffic brought the range to 3·8-4·8 per cent. Benefits of leisure-time savings raised the rates (at 20p per hour) to 5·4-7·1 per cent and (at 40p per hour) to 7·0-9·4 per cent. Further calculations based on elaborate estimates of traffic growth in the economy generally placed the returns by 1965 in the region of 17·6-27·3 per cent on the original capital cost.

Reservations and criticisms

The results of the motorway study suggest it is feasible in principle to appraise the benefits óf road construction in this way. But two reservations are essential. The original report contains ingenious analysis, *but also arbitrary assumptions.* Applying similar sets of assumptions to various road programmes would be a valuable means of choosing priorities and exploring the benefits of differing scales of development of routes. For some time at least the benefits obtained through the construction of the M1 could have been matched by a more modest two-lane dual carriageway.[2]

[1] Mainly from Sweden and the United States.
[2] The US practice of matching incremental (marginal) benefits of a larger-scale project against its incremental (marginal) costs will be recalled.

Where choice of priorities affected various parts of the country it would naturally have to be assumed that the unit value of benefits to one area were equal, pound for pound, with those elsewhere. This is a proposition which no amount of analysis can deny. Perhaps more important, however, is that the Road Research Laboratory were interested in obtaining a rate-of-return criterion not only to facilitate choice between alternative road investments but also between roads and other classes of investment. Was their analysis successful? This problem has provoked a most interesting and important debate.

Briefly, the rates of return in private industry, which must to some degree set the tone in the market for investment funds, are based on the actions of profit-maximising firms. The benefits which consumers derive from an investment are reflected in the total value of consumers' expenditure, by 'price times quantity'. This figure does not represent the total satisfaction obtained by consumers. For example, any consumer who would have bought some units of the goods in question at a higher price will, if the price is lowered, be obtaining goods for a reduced outlay. In technical language consumption is pushed to a point where marginal utility is equated with price, with intra-marginal units giving more satisfaction than the cost of obtaining them. This is the notion of 'consumers surplus' made famous by Alfred Marshall.[1]

It has been argued by Mr D. W. Glassborow[2] that the methods used in the motorway study are such that the primary magnitude estimated is total satisfaction or utility. There is nothing inherently wrong in this method since the investment is so large as to bring about a fundamental rather than marginal change in the transport facilities available. There is thus an 'indivisibility' problem (above, page 22). Mr Glassborow's major concern, however, arises from the likelihood that the Road Research Laboratory's practice would automatically generate an estimate of the rate of return (total consumers' satisfaction expressed as a percentage of capital cost) from road construction likely to exceed the returns calculated for rail improvements. It is therefore necessary to see how the latter are now calculated.

Given a rail improvement (an electrification scheme, for example), users of the enhanced facilities would be required to pay fares in line with the route charges per mile of the railway system as a whole. The scheme would then be approved or rejected by a financial calculation (total net revenue set against capital costs). A time- and cost-saving calculation of the type used by the Road Research Laboratory, by attempting to value the total worth of the scheme rather than the total revenue, would almost certainly show a higher return. In other words, the rail authorities would not extract the total value of additional satisfaction: the 'consumers' surplus'

[1] *Principles of Economics,* 8th edn., Macmillan, 1952, especially Book III, Ch. VI.

[2] 'The Road Research Laboratory's Investment Criterion Examined', *Bulletin of the Oxford University Institute of Statistics,* November 1960. Comments by M. E. Beesley, 'Mr. Glassborow on Investment Criteria', are contained in the May 1961 issue.

would be omitted.[1] From his researches Mr Glassborow quoted examples of improvements to suburban services yielding 7 to 10 per cent on an accounting basis, but up to 30 per cent when valued by Road Research Laboratory methods.

If the 'rates of return' calculated from the cost-benefit study of road improvements are accepted at their face value, there is a danger of applying a dual standard of appraisal to competing investments. The risk of misallocating resources in favour of road improvements is blatant. It has not escaped the attention of transport economists who favour a cost-benefit approach. Mr Foster, for example, argued that there is an obvious need for 'co-ordination' of competing services and that standardised methods should be used.[2] Even then there would remain the problem of charging. The use of roads and railways (and the returns likely to arise from improvements in them) is clearly dependent upon the policy adopted in fixing rates for public transport and upon the types of taxes imposed upon road users. The task of designing a tax system and a structure of rates and fares consistent with each other remains.[3] It is of enormous importance, not least in the study of the Victoria Line (below, p. 33).

A closely related principle is raised by Dr Mishan.[4] Consider a proposal for improving a route on which there is serious congestion but no road-pricing device which imputes to travellers the marginal (external) social cost they impose on others. Benefits from the improvement will include, *inter alia*, reduced travel time and operating costs. The size of benefits may be quoted in order to judge the scheme in the order of priority for road improvement and often to justify the worthwhileness of the investment *per se* in relation to investment in other activities. In both cases, however, there is a defect in the argument. Suppose road pricing were introduced to achieve an 'optimal traffic flow' with road charges being equated to marginal congestion costs. Charges would probably reduce the flow of traffic: some users would be unwilling to pay the price of congestion as indicated by a market mechanism and

[1] Extracting as payment the total value of consumers' satisfaction would involve price discrimination—perhaps by charging higher rates for peak-hour travel. It could be economically difficult to arrange such a system (and perhaps politically infeasible).

[2] C. D. Foster, 'Surplus Criteria for Investment', *Bulletin of the Oxford University Institute of Statistics*, November 1960. For detailed critiques of the concept of 'co-ordination', A. A. Walters, *Integration in Freight Transport*, Research Monograph 15, IEA, 1968, and G. J. Ponsonby, *Transport Policy: Co-ordination through Competition*, Hobart Paper 49, IEA, 1969.

[3] For extended discussion, Foster, *ibid.*, and *The Transport Problem, op. cit.*, especially Ch. 10. Put briefly Foster's recommendations are that rail fares should cover average costs (including an interest charge based on a 'rough value-judgement' of what returns should be earned in transport), and that road users should pay through taxes the average cost of road provision. Choice between investments would then be possible on the basis of the Road Research Laboratory methods described above, and those used in the Victoria Line study (below). It should be noted that this is not equivalent to the profit-maximising policies of private businesses. There is no criterion by which transport investments can be judged against the general level of interest rates. D. G. Tipping, 'Consumers' Surplus in Public Enterprise', *The Manchester School*, September 1966, provides a detailed criticism of consumers' surplus criteria (mainly on the ground of the difficulties of measurement).

[4] *The Costs of Economic Growth, op. cit.*, Appendix C: 'A Note on the Interpretation of the Benefits of Private Transport', reprinted from *Journal of Transport Economics and Policy*, May 1966.

would seek transport by rail or bus. The basic question now is: Why give weight to the benefits of road improvement accruing to those who would not pay the price of road space if they had to do so through road charges? The typical cost-benefit calculation includes *all* time and cost savings, regardless of willingness to pay.

Two conclusions emerge. The first is that, if the difficult task of valuing benefits not directly reflected in the market is attempted (and this process lies at the heart of cost-benefit analysis), the results could conceivably be an incorrect guide to action.[1] Secondly, many writers have proposed re-organising the financing of road provision by marginal social cost charging.[2] Such proposals would by no means be easy to implement since they would require complex methods of using taxes on vehicles (excise licences and fuel taxes, for example) to reflect marginal costs to the road user, and might also involve some form of direct charging (through metering devices) on congested routes. Additionally (as in cost-benefit studies), forecasting changes in traffic flows resulting from the construction of new roads would be difficult. In principle, however, such charges would provide a means of appraising investment. Benefits would be more closely reflected by payments, and calculated rates of return more easily comparable with those earned in other activities would be obtained. Technically cost-benefit analysis, of the type carried out by the Road Research Laboratory in the M1 study, might then be redundant.[3]

(b) The Victoria Line study. Cost-benefit methods are advocated for dealing with projects in which either investments are large and indivisible, group wants are catered for, prices are not charged to consumers for the use of final output, or important externality effects exist. In their study of the Victoria Line Mr C. D. Foster and Professor Michael Beesley recognised these factors but emphasised that there were other overwhelming reasons for attempting a cost-benefit analysis of the project.[4] Viewed by London Transport as a purely commercial venture, the Victoria Line was not attractive. The new line, according to the estimates quoted by Foster and Beesley, was unlikely to earn enough at the current fares to meet running costs, depreciation and interest charges. The deficit was estimated at £2·14 million per year

[1] For example, it has been stated that the proposed construction of a London 'motorway box', at a cost of some £860 million, would give benefits of the order of 20 per cent per annum, largely as a result of reducing congestion costs. (Letter to *The Times*, 10 February, 1968, by Mr Robert Vigars of the Greater London Council.) The implication that the investment seems to be easily justifiable should be scrutinised in the light of the discussion by Mr Glassborow and Dr Mishan.

[2] Above, p. 21; also Gabriel Roth, *A Self-financing Road System,* Research Monograph 3, IEA, 1966: his views on cost-benefit analysis are in pp. 37-39.

[3] The sentence is written in this form since non-marginal investments would remain to be appraised (i.e., indivisibilities could arise). In this case elements of 'consumers' surplus' should be included. But the whole exercise would be based on a system of charging having a firm economic foundation. (Mishan, *passim.*)

[4] C. D. Foster and M. E. Beesley, 'Estimating the Social Benefit of Constructing an Underground Railway in London', *Journal of the Royal Statistical Society*, Series A, Vol. 126, Part 1, 1963.

(at a charge of 6 per cent interest on capital costs) on the Line and £3·12 million to London Transport because of consequent losses of revenue from other services. If the financial rate of return, *at the existing fares,* were the deciding factor the Line would not have been built.

This state of affairs was stated to be a consequence of the illogical pricing of transport in cities. Two factors were noted. For a financial calculation to indicate that an investment is profitable (and therefore that it would be an efficient use of resources), prices should reflect the value consumers place on the services. In London, however, government decree and the Transport Tribunal have resulted in fares well below the market rates that would be charged by a profit-maximising operator. It is not surprising that, given such interference, the commercial viability of the Line should be questionable. In the second place there is a marked dichotomy between the treatment of public transport and private road users. The former may at least come near to covering average costs of operation through the fares they pay: the latter pay a price which in no way reflects the real costs of their travel. The argument runs that a marginal social cost pricing policy for road users would cause a significant shift towards public transport and a consequent transformation of its finances.

This amounts to saying that a cost-benefit analysis of the Victoria Line becomes necessary only as a second-best exercise given that market prices were currently distorted and did not therefore reflect the points of highest profitability: price distortion had frustrated the market's function as an allocator of scarce resources.

Measurement of benefits thus involved indirect evaluation. Here Foster and Beesley argued that three broad groups of 'benefit' should be taken into consideration. First, traffic diverted to the Victoria Line from other travel modes would reap direct advantages in time-savings, added comfort and convenience, and private motorists would gain economies in vehicle operating costs. Second, traffic not diverted to the Victoria Line would benefit indirectly mainly as a result of the new facility speeding up the flow of surface transport with savings in time and vehicle operating costs (an external effect). Third, benefits would accrue to those who would find it worthwhile, because of shorter journey times, to undertake trips which might not otherwise have been made; this was the benefit to 'generated traffic'. The problems which then arose consisted of measuring the physical impact of construction (e.g. how much traffic would be diverted, how much weight was to be given to the externality effects on surface transport, how much traffic would be generated), and of placing a money value on each of the features recorded. Some of these difficulties of physical estimation would confront any economic appraisal of a new underground route. An efficient pricing structure would enable only the second part of the exercise— valuation—to be undertaken with more precision. As matters stood, however, the fares to be paid were ignored, the calculation proceeding on lines very similar to those adopted in the M1 study.

Imputation of values to time-savings

A large part of the work in assembling these physical estimates was undertaken by London Transport, the effects on road use being quantified by complex models of road traffic behaviour developed by the Road Research Laboratory. The imputation of values to some items merits discussion.

Many of the benefits related to time-savings, so two valuations, for working- and for non-working-time travel, were adopted. The former could be assessed using a sample-based estimate of hourly rates of pay. Here, however, the bulk of the problem remained unresolved since it was estimated that 95 per cent of time-savings would occur in non-working hours. In this case the choice of value (25p per hour) was again, as the authors remarked, 'arbitrary but not perhaps unreasonable'.[1]

Comfort and convenience were estimated by an indirect route. Given the valuation of time it was argued that, by observation of people faced with a choice between fast services (with low probability of seating) and slow services (with a higher probability of seating), a value could be set on the rate of substitution of comfort for time; hence comfort factors could be imputed. Finally, as for the M1 study, some trends were assumed to accommodate growth in demand for transport facilities.

Table I brings together a selection of the final results. This Table illustrates the crucial step in a cost-benefit analysis, the final appraisal. Foster and Beesley compared the value of capital expenditure with the discounted value of benefits occurring through an assumed 50-year operating life of the project. This was a more sophisticated approach than the calculation of the crude rate of return on capital in the M1 study. The rate of discount chosen for use in the Table, since it resulted in benefits exceeding costs, implied that returns of more than 6 per cent on the capital employed could be expected. (Benefits would still exceed costs using a discount rate of 8 per cent.)[2]

---

[1] Readers particularly interested in problems of valuation might consult Professor Beesley's 'The Value of Time Spent in Travelling: Some New Evidence', *Economica*, May 1965. This neat study related to the travel behaviour of a sample of civil servants working in central London. Evidence was collected by questionnaire relating to the time and cost of both preferred modes of travel to work and of the next best alternative. After elimination of inconsistent replies (for example, cases in which a slower and more costly mode was chosen instead of faster, cheaper travel) a 'trade-off' was established between 'time' and 'cost'. The results gave values from 10p to 16p per hour, and appeared to be dependent on income levels. It was suggested that travel time (on an hourly basis) could be valued at approximately one-third of hourly pay (but see below, pp. 52-3, 55). Note that the substitution of values in this range would reduce the 'total benefits less running costs' attributable to the Victoria Line (below, Table I) to approximately £52 million. This estimate still exceeds the investment cost.

[2] In their original paper Foster and Beesley adopted the additional practice of expressing the difference between total discounted benefits less running costs (£69·71 million) and capital expenditure itself, averaged over the whole period of construction and operation of the line. Those particularly interested in the intricacies of discounting might refer to subsequent discussion of the paper by J. M. Thomson and D. L. Munby where the logic of this procedure and the outcome of the calculations were questioned. (*Journal of the Royal Statistical Society*, Vol. 126, Part I, 1963, pp. 84-5, 88-92.)

TABLE I

Social Benefits from the Victoria Line

		Annual amount £ m.	Present value at 6% discount £ m.
Costs			
A. Annual working costs		1·413	16·16
Benefits			
B. Traffic diverted to V.L.			
(1) Underground: Time		·378	4·32
Comfort		·347	3·96
(2) British Railways: Time		·205	2·93
(3) Buses: Time		·575	6·58
(4) Motorists: Time		·153	3·25
Cost		·377	8·02
(5) Pedestrians: Time		·020	·28
	Sub-Total	2·055	29·34
C. Traffic not diverted			
	Sub-Total	3·916	44·79
D. Generated traffic			
	Sub-Total	·822	11·74
Total Benefits			85·87
Total Benefits less running costs			69·71
Value of Capital Expenditure			38·81

Source: C. D. Foster and M. E. Beesley, *op. cit.,* p. 49. The present discounted values are based on the annual amounts for each item amended where appropriate for trend factors. Discounting is, of course, very similar to calculating compound interest. If the interest rate is 3 per cent then £100 today is worth £100 × 1·03 = £103 a year hence, and £100 × 1·03² = £106·09 two years hence. Similarly £106·09 available two years hence at 3 per cent *discount* is worth £100 today.

Implications for transport policy

Only two points remain for discussion. First, the authors did not attempt to take the full social consequences of building the Victoria Line into consideration. It is often held—probably rightly—that the improvement of transport facilities in major conurbations, especially where fare levels are subsidised, may induce extra growth of population. Congestion, and its consequent social costs, may be temporarily relieved only to require the expenditure of vast sums of money sooner or later to repeat the same process. If as a general aim we are, for instance, interested in diverting office employment from the London area, the construction of facilities which make London more attractive to firms and office workers cannot be counted as wholly beneficial. Indeed the two programmes are quite obviously in direct conflict with each other, and the omission of such consequences on the ground that they are indirect or unquantifiable can hardly be held to promote clarity in policy formation. Valuing benefits to generated traffic, as well as building trend estimates into the calculations, becomes a doubtful step when viewed in this light.

Secondly, it is important to reiterate that both the M1 and Victoria Line calculations were undertaken against the background of current vehicle taxes and fares and in the absence of an attempt to charge user prices, by congestion taxes, to ration scarce road space. There would be substantial differences between the results of a cost-benefit analysis of transport investment under the present non-pricing policy for the use of road space and after improvements had been made in the underlying structure of charging.[1]

[1] Readers interested in the effects of alternative charging systems on the consumers' surplus rate of return of the Victoria line might consult M. E. Beesley and C. D. Foster, 'The Victoria Line: Social Benefit and Finances', *Journal of the Royal Statistical Society,* Vol. 128, Part 1, 1965; also the discussion above, pp. 33-34.

IV Applications to Land-use and Town Planning Problems

In advocating cost-benefit techniques, Professor Hall saw regional development and the detailed planning of cities as a major area for their application.[1] What progress has been made in Britain in recent years?

A. Land Conservation

The conservation of land for agricultural use is of the first importance in a crowded island such as Britain with a growing population heavily dependent for its food supplies on overseas producers. In cost-benefit methodology few major valuation problems are raised except in the choice of a discounting factor. Since urban development constantly runs up against the conservation of agricultural land, a brief review of the underlying food supply position and the capacity of British agriculture to meet it forms an appropriate starting point for inquiry.

The analysis, recently completed by Mrs A. M. Edwards and Professor G. P. Wibberley,[2] focusses on the year 2000, by which time it is expected that transfer of agricultural land to other uses (notably urban development and afforestation) will have reduced land for farming by 7·64 per cent (3·7 million acres). In 1965 (the base year of the study) some 48·5 million acres were in agricultural use. When adjustments are made for land quality, the loss of productive potential is placed at some 9·65 per cent of 1965 levels. Estimates of the growth in demand for domestic agricultural output allowing for possible variation in the rates of population and income growth and for changes in the degree of self-sufficiency in food supply (the analysis was confined to 'temperate latitude' products) were coupled with projections of the rate of growth in agricultural output per acre. On this basis Mrs Edwards and Professor Wibberley were able to investigate the potential effects on the 'land budget' of a variety of possibilities. To illustrate but one of their examples, they were able to show that growth in population of 0·65 per cent per annum, with income growing at 2·5 per cent per annum, would generate increased food demand of 36·6 per cent by 2000. If self-sufficiency rose from 60 per cent in 1965 to 75 per cent the aggregate increase would be transformed into a rise in demand for domestic output of 71 per cent. Nevertheless an expansion in output per acre at a compound rate of 2 per cent per annum (which would double production over a 35-year period) could accommodate

---

[1] Hall, *loc. cit.*, p. 174.
[2] A. M. Edwards and G. P. Wibberley, *An Agricultural Land Budget for Britain, 1965-2000*, Studies in Rural Land Use No. 10, Wye College, University of London, 1971.

this increase and leave a margin of almost 5 per cent of the land area above the forecast loss of 9·65 per cent of agricultural potential. A self-sufficiency of almost 80 per cent (which should satisfy even those who take a grossly pessimistic view of Britain's trading prospects) could be met if the other assumptions were left unchanged.

The growth rates of population, income and output per acre used above appear to be realistic projections. The implication is that a serious conflict between agricultural and urban land use is unlikely to occur unless a vast change is required in self-sufficiency. Given such an outlook there appears to be little warrant for rigidly conserving agricultural land at the expense of higher urban residential densities, though for reasons of caution urban expansion might be directed, when possible, to areas of lower agricultural value. Since land quality in Britain can vary rapidly over short distances a wholesale shifting of centres of development is not necessary; but choice of available sites should be scrutinised, especially where major expansion, such as the creation of new towns, is contemplated.

Factors other than land quality must also be drawn into the equation. By its very nature, good agricultural land is likely to be that on which building operations, especially as reflected in the costs of basic site works, are easier. Economising good quality land, in short, is likely to confront Britain with increasing cost of urban development. Two sides of the coin need to be considered.[1]

Valuation of farm land

The agricultural value of land is represented by the pure economic rent of land alone, given by the total value of output less the costs of all non-land factors used in production. However, if the services of other immobile assets (notably farm buildings in this case) are also lost, their annual value must be added to the land-value figure. It might be expected that the total could be estimated simply by a survey of farm rents, though such a solution would not necessarily be reliable since for many years farm rents have been prevented by law from reaching free-market levels. The value to society cannot be adequately reflected *via* a market distorted by government control. It requires indirect analysis.[2]

The process of estimation entails a survey of possible development sites, valuation of total output and deduction of the relevant costs. Here the most difficult problems are, first, that if market rentals are low the difference between the current and the free-market rents must accrue to some other factor of production. Farm incomes may rise to more than farmers would accept as an adequate long-run reward, and

---

[1] G. P. Wibberley, *Agriculture and Urban Growth*, Michael Joseph, 1959.

[2] This raises a general proposition in cost-benefit analysis: if market values are taken to reflect 'social' values one must be certain that the market is allowed to work smoothly. The term 'shadow price' is frequently used to denote an adjusted market price of a commodity or factor of production. It is also extended to cover cases in which a hypothetical valuation is placed upon a good or service not 'sold' in the market.

the true opportunity cost of farm enterprise would then be over-stated. Alternatively, the costs of inputs (e.g. fertilisers and machinery) may be driven upwards. Second, agriculture receives support which raises farm prices above free-market levels. Whether this policy is in the national interest is a question on which economists differ. It was certainly arguable that our method of subsidising product prices raised internal prices above the true opportunity costs of obtaining agricultural products, as reflected by import prices. This, in turn, would result in an over-valuation of the services of agricultural land since product prices are an important determinant of rents.[1]

Discounting for social preferences

In the early work on this subject the analysis was set up in the following way. Assume that two prospective sites, of different land quality, are being considered for urban development and that their respective annual agricultural values and the comparative costs of basic site preparation are known. It is here that the discounting problem arises. Capital costs are once-and-for-all; agricultural value accrues as a time-stream of annual receipts. Suppose the 'good' site has a larger agricultural value (R) than that of the poorer site, while the extra capital costs (C) which would be involved in developing the poorer in preference to the better are also known.[2] If the capitalised value of R is higher than C the poorer site appears preferable for development. But in order to capitalise, some judgement must be made on the 'social' rate of time preference. If *future* benefits are desired markedly less than *present* satisfactions (a high discount factor) the value of R capitalised would be lower than in the opposite case. In the original studies it was argued that *private* rates of discount appropriate to investments in agricultural land are indicated immediately by comparing farm rental values with the market-determined capital value of farm property. At that time (1959) this resulted in an estimate of approximately 4 per cent. Is this an appropriate method for making what is essentially a *social* decision?

Professor Wibberley argued that it is not, and he substantiated his claim by evidence from Holland. In that country the capital costs of reclaiming land are roughly twice the value for which the resulting farms can be sold; alternatively, the social rate of discount is half the private rate. Since the decision to reclaim, in face of the known

---

[1] The problems in determining the true 'shadow price' of agricultural output are discussed in G. H. Peters, 'Land Use Studies in Britain: A Review of the Literature with Special Reference to Applications of Cost-Benefit Analysis', *Journal of Agricultural Economics*, May 1970. In most studies the researchers have simply valued output at subsidised prices. For future work it can be noted that Britain's accession to the EEC, and adoption of the common agricultural policy, will result in the opportunity cost of farm products being best represented by support prices, for there will no longer be a gap between the prices received by domestic farmers and the cost of imports.

[2] Wibberley, *op. cit.*, Ch. 10, considers the comparative advantage of proposed extensions to the Manchester housing area at Lymm and Moberley. Other examples are given by J. T. Ward, 'The Siting of Urban Development in Agricultural Land', *Journal of Agricultural Economics*, December 1957.

facts, is sanctioned by the electorate, he argued that it might provide an indicator for British policy. He also pointed out that we too are prepared to grant capital for farm improvements (notably in upland areas) which raise the capital value of farm property, on sale, by only about one-half of the value of the sums expended. Clearly, a *social* rate of discount in the appraisal arrived at by halving the private rate would substantially reinforce the argument for preserving better-quality land in agricultural use.

Though this argument may appear compelling, it must also be asked whether the 'private' discount rate is itself appropriate as a base-line from which to work.[1] The elements of C (additional costs of site works) are related to the costs of using real resources to secure a future return. Thus it is a measure of the opportunity cost of capital which appears to be more appropriate as a base-line than the rate of discount established within the land market *per se*.[2]

Professors Wibberley and Ward set out their analytic method to attempt to cope with a comparatively simple situation. However, the value of agricultural land frequently appears as one of many items which may need to be estimated in planning studies. There is an interesting discussion of the correct basis for evaluation in the final report of the Roskill Commission.[3] Here a group of interested parties sought to argue that the annual value of land should be measured by taking the gross value of output and deducting only the value of such non-agricultural intermediate inputs as fertiliser, fuel, feed and seed. To do so, however, would have been to take the whole of agricultural 'value added' (i.e., the incomes of *all* factors of production in farming use) as an estimate of the contribution of land plus immobile physical assets. The Commission quickly accepted the view of Professor Wibberley and Mr M. Boddington, who insisted that the correct basis for valuation should include the worth only of land and fixed assets. As a discount factor they then employed a value of 10 per cent as in all other items in the appraisal (below, p. 51 and Table III). They made no attempt to use an adjusted 'social' rate; nor did they question the initial valuation of output at support prices.

Flats to save land?

It is often argued that building flats might in the last analysis save agricultural land. This view is not supported by the work of Dr P. A. Stone. His general conclusion is that the economics of high building are such that land savings are made only at very high capital costs.[4] In summary his results indicated that it cost £21,500 (at 1964

---

[1] Peters, *loc. cit.*

[2] The capital value of land can be affected by estate duty concessions, speculation in anticipated capital gains, the prestige of ownership, and so on. They all lower the private rate of discount.

[3] Commission on the Third London Airport, *Report*, HMSO, 1971, Appendix 9.

[4] *Urban Development in Britain: Standards, Costs and Revenues 1964-2004*, Cambridge University Press, 1970, Vol. 1, p. 157. These estimates are somewhat lower than in his 'The Economics of Housing and Urban Development', *Journal of the Royal Statistical Society*, Vol. 122, Part 4, 1959, and *Housing, Town Development, Land and Costs*, The Estates Gazette, 1963.

prices) to 'save' one acre of agricultural land (valued in the market in 1964 at about £250 per acre) by raising the height of buildings from two storeys to four. Ten-storeyed structures, in comparison with the conventional house, involved additional costs of £44,000 for each acre saved.

B. Urban Development: Cost-Benefit Alternatives

(i) *The Buchanan Approach*

Though the examples of cost-benefit analysis so far refer to vastly different basic issues they have one important feature in common: the benefits have been valued in money. Two results follow. First, the relative merits of two or more projects designed for a similar purpose can be compared. Secondly, the economic wisdom of choosing any project, as opposed to using funds elsewhere for different purposes, may in some circumstances be rationally assessed in money. If part of the costs must be met by public subsidy there is at least some approximate assurance that commensurate economic benefits are being obtained.

The steps in making a thoroughgoing cost-benefit study of this nature require assessment of benefits, with non-marketed services being imputed a 'shadow price', and a technique for measuring rates of return. The success of such efforts depends upon a suitable means of shadow pricing. The method cannot otherwise be applied in its most highly developed form.

Cost-benefit analysis was applied as a laboratory experiment in the Buchanan Report to three alternative schemes for the development of Newbury.[1] Benefit evaluation was concerned largely with assessing the value of non-marketable services. The implications of the Buchanan Report raised the question whether the cost of implementing it would be worth paying. Though the Report was not very explicit in its estimation of the likely total costs, an independent estimate by Mr Foster put the figure, over a 20-year period, at £18,000 million.[2] This estimate was derived from the costs of intermediate-scale re-development as envisaged by Buchanan for Newbury, Norwich, Leeds and part of central London, applied to all towns of over 20,000 population.

The three schemes of re-development considered in the Report involved costs of refurbishing the transport network which rose to a maximum of £5·6 million, after deduction of potential re-development values likely to be generated by each scheme.

The benefits accruing from each scheme are set out in Table II. For vehicle users the main gain was largely one of accessibility. For others the nature of the environment, including safety (defined as the extent to which there is separation of pedestrians and vehicles), comfort (proximity of pedestrian areas or buildings to heavy vehicle

---

[1] *Traffic in Towns, loc. cit.*, Appendix 2.
[2] C. D. Foster, 'Can we afford Buchanan?', *Statist*, 28 February, 1964.

TABLE II A
The Newbury Study—Benefits and Costs

Schemes	Index of Environmental Accessibility	Benefit	Cost £ m.	Benefit / Cost
No change	11	—	0·0	—
A	22	11	2·7	4·1
B	57	46	3·4	13·5
C	72	61	5·6	10·9

Table IIB shows the incremental benefits and costs derived from Table II A.

TABLE II B
The Newbury Study—Incremental Benefits and Costs

Schemes	Benefit	Cost £ m.	Benefit / Cost
A	11	2·7	4
B	35	0·7	50
C	15	2·2	7

flows), convenience (access to public transport) and appearance (the extent of parked vehicles) were the important factors. The benefits, in short, were more or less intangible and monetary measurement of satisfaction was regarded as impossible. Instead it was decided to use an arbitrarily-determined scale to obtain a subjective valuation of the effects of each scheme, and to compare each with the likely consequences of taking no action. The index of 'environmental accessibility' so determined was used as a scale for measuring benefits to be set against the computed costs.[1] The maximum increase in benefits is achieved by adopting the most costly scheme (scheme C in Table II A), though the maximum *ratio* of benefits to costs is achieved by the less ambitious scheme B.

The results of the exercise indicate that though maximum benefit is obtained in scheme C, the increase in benefit over scheme B is comparatively low in relation to the additional cost. As a town-planning device, the formulation of the problem in this way may be a useful tool. It has, however, been forcibly pointed out by Professor Beesley and Mr J. F. Kain that drawing up arbitrary scales of effectiveness and weighting them together into an overall index is tantamount to the analysts 'dressing

---

[1] Here we are dealing with what might be called a 'cost of effectiveness' study rather than with thoroughgoing cost-benefit analysis.

up their own prejudices'.[1] Although the Buchanan Report emphasised that investment decisions relating to total public investment needed for town improvement and to its allocation between specific projects must be taken, it is proving extremely difficult to formulate cost-benefit techniques appropriate to guiding the total allocation decision.

The Newbury study yielded a crude measure of the advantages, in relation to cost, of various possible schemes. But a cost-effectiveness study, using a non-monetary scale of benefits, cannot form the basis of a thorough-going investment appraisal.

(ii) *The Planning Balance-Sheet Approach*

Further attempts to grapple with the problem of choice in town development have been initiated by Professor N. Lichfield, who was responsible for the cost-benefit work in the Buchanan Report. His studies of Cambridge and Swanley are major steps in his attempt to evolve a standard form of appraisal.[2] In both exercises, and in others which are unpublished, the method employed differs substantially from the cost-effectiveness approach which uses an arbitrary index of benefits to set against money costs. Lichfield analyses the costs and benefits of alternative town developments as they affect a wide range of interests. The 'standard form' of balance sheet outlines the repercussions on 'Producers and Operators' who initiate and execute the scheme and on 'Consumers' who use the services. Under the first head the local authority is assumed to foster development notably by acquiring land, constructing public works and buildings, and creating ground leases for private developers. 'Landowners', who may or may not be displaced by the development, will also be affected. The 'consumers' include the occupiers of new houses, shops, offices and dwellings, and of new public buildings, as well as motor-vehicle users, the shopping public and the public at large. Previous residential or business occupiers of buildings (as opposed to landowners) must also be considered whether they are displaced or not. With them, and also non-displaced landowners, the basic problem concerns the extent to which externalities affecting their living conditions, and the capital values of their property, might be important. Complex analysis sheets are employed as accounts of costs and benefits, containing entries under roughly 20 major sub-headings with further breakdowns in each. A balance is attempted for each sub-heading to select the most advantageous scheme.

[1] 'Urban Form, Car Ownership and Public Policy, An Appraisal of Traffic in Towns', *Urban Studies*, November 1964.

[2] *Cost Benefit Analysis in Town Planning: A case study of Cambridge*, Cambridge and Isle of Ely County Council, 1966, reprinted in J. Margolis (ed.), *The Public Economy of Urban Communities*, Oxford University Press, 1966; also 'Cost Benefit Analysis in Town Planning—a case study: Swanley', *Urban Studies*, November 1967. A listing of unpublished studies in Worthing, Stevenage and Ipswich is given in 'Economics in Town Planning', *Town Planning Review*, April 1968. A study of Peterborough is in *Regional Studies*, September 1969. A general review is in 'Evaluation Methodology of Urban and Regional Plans', *Regional Studies*, August 1970.

A monetary evaluation of costs and benefits is given under very few of the headings. Indeed the only major attempts at such evaluation are the construction costs of each scheme (whether incurred by the local authority or private developers), the estimated annual values of rental income likely to be generated, and the value of the compensation payments to displaced people. From this analysis some idea can be gained of the value of the real resources required, and of the transfer payments. But one is then asked to consider them in relation to a long list of benefits and costs to various interest groups for which only an impressionistic and qualitative ranking is available.[1] Though in Cambridge the answers obtained were fairly clear-cut it was emphasised in the Swanley study that there was no obvious balance of advantage either way and consequently there was much room for value-judgement, particularly in inter-personal comparisons.[2] The advantages claimed by Professor Lichfield are that his approach at least lays bare the basis for value-judgements and presents a comprehensive picture which makes it difficult to assess aspects of planning proposals out of context.

Weaknesses of the alternative methods (Lichfield v. Buchanan)

Unfortunately, in their attempts to evolve methods of guidance the town planners appear to be caught between two stools. In Professor Lichfield's studies, as they now stand, one is bombarded with information and invited to judge the relative merits of alternative schemes. Monetary measures, quantitative measures and qualitative judgements are superimposed one upon the other in a somewhat confusing array. No single indicator can be grasped. In the Buchanan Report, on the other hand, the points-scoring system does aim to produce an overall index of benefits, although based essentially on the value-judgements of the analysts to which anyone might justifiably object. The end-results are simple to interpret, but it is a pseudo-simplicity which masks the basic components of the analysis. There appears to be no easy way out of this *impasse*. The impression remains that an onerous amount of work has produced no clear-cut result.

The later analysis seems open to more fundamental criticism. There is a danger of 'double counting'. In discussing the values of commercial properties, for example, Professor Lichfield attempts a rough evaluation of the rental incomes which might be commanded after the completion of re-development. This is one monetary item in his balance sheets. At the same time he includes a weighing of other advantages, such as ease of movement for pedestrians and vehicles, within the analysis. The value

---

[1] Examples are the changes in potential development value, freedom of traffic flow, absence of accidents, ease of car parking, the convenience of shopping, noise, architectural form, general surroundings, reduction of the influence of motor vehicles on environment, and, in the case of Cambridge, the maintenance of the dominant role of the University in the city's life. The study emphasised that there may be scope in some cases for measurement either in monetary or physical units, but that in others intangibles are involved.

[2] It is envisaged that the results would be presented to local authorities as a basis for decisions. They might also feature in public inquiries and could conceivably be put to the voters.

of commercial property is vitally affected by accessibility. The components are not in principle separable: what are in essence private advantages to the developers and occupiers of commercial buildings are to some degree at least indicators of wider social benefits. The argument suffers from an embarrassing degree of circularity.

These objections have been taken up by Mr William Lean[1] who suggests that changes in aggregate land values, assessed over wide areas, might be a useful way of comparing the results of alternative forms of development, maximisation of land values providing a key to the relative merits of opposing schemes. Mr Lean clearly believes that the land market can reflect a wide range of benefits in an adequate and telling way and that it should be relied upon as a basic indicator. This, of course, is to a large degree true if one considers society's preferences as between land uses at the margin. But re-development schemes are far from marginal changes, and may cause such fundamental re-alignments in land values that valuation techniques would be strained to the limit in appraising the consequences. It is a most discouraging situation in which economists seem able to provide little explicit guidance to physical land-use planners.

Dearth of urban re-development studies

Apart from Professor Lichfield there appear to be few English researchers in urban cost-benefit problems whose analyses are easily accessible. An interesting study by Messrs Flowerdew and Stannard has emerged from the Planning Department of the Greater London Council.[2] It considered four alternative proposals for re-developing the Kings Reach area on the South Bank of the Thames between Waterloo and Blackfriars Bridges. The authors recognised that the task could be tackled by the Lichfield method, but their study was less wide-ranging. It analysed the advantages to the local authority and private developers of plans with varying intensities of land use and argued that, to such operators, there would be distinct (private) advantages in intensive re-development. These were then set against calculated costs of traffic congestion which would also be expected to be higher as densities rose, a variable for which Professor Lichfield did not attempt monetary evaluation. The analysis was an exercise in forecasting traffic generation, based on its relationship with land-use intensity, and in measuring the marginal social cost of congestion to private road users by the Smeed formula.[3] There was no consideration of congestion costs imposed on public transport. The results, which were presented only in outline, suggest that a modest 'thinning out' of development might be worthwhile, but that for more drastic

[1] *Economics of Land Use Planning: Urban and Regional,* The Estates Gazette, London, 1969.
[2] A. D. J. Flowerdew and R. B. Stannard, *Cost Benefit Analysis in Central London Re-Development,* papers delivered at the Urban Studies Conference, Oxford, September 1967.
[3] *Road Pricing: The Economic and Technical Possibilities, op. cit.,* p. 17. Colin Clark, *Population and Land Use,* Macmillan, 1967, especially Ch. IX, discusses pricing and much else relevant to the economics of urban areas.

schemes the cuts in congestion costs would not outweigh financial losses, particularly to the local authority.

C. Town Expansions versus New Towns

Another important aspect of town planning concerns the relative merits of town expansion (in which an existing settlement is made the focal point for growth in population) and 'new town' development. During the 1960s considerable work was sponsored by the then Ministry of Housing and Local Government. It commissioned studies relating, *inter alia*, to expansion schemes for Worcester, Peterborough and Ipswich, in which estimates were made of the resource costs of major expansions to cater for increased population. Dr Stone was also engaged in similar work.[1] The results were neatly summarised by the South-East Joint Planning Team in its work on the Strategic Plan for the South-East completed in 1970.[2] The general conclusions were that the unit costs of new town formation (including housing, roads, shopping facilities, public buildings, etc.) are just over £2,000 per head of population, at a population level of 50,000, rising only slowly thereafter. By contrast, the *per capita* costs of town expansions (assuming an initial base level of 50,000 population) fall quite sharply up to population sizes of 150,000 and then remain more or less constant for larger-scale expansions up to 250,000. In the range of population sizes from 150,000 upwards new town formation appears to retain some cost advantage, though this is of marginal significance.[3]

These costing studies refer only to initial construction; they do not explore the costs of maintaining the urban fabric or of operating local services.[4] Furthermore they cannot be described as applications of cost-benefit analysis. The South-East Joint Planning Team emphasised that a minimum-cost solution to providing accommodation and urban services is not necessarily optimal since the benefits of urban development of a given size, location or form are themselves variable. Increased size may, for example, improve job opportunities, extend the range of social contacts

[1] Stone (1970), *op. cit.*

[2] South-East Joint Planning Team, *Strategic Plan for the South-East: Studies, Volume 4: Strategies and Evaluation*, HMSO, 1971, Ch. 7.

[3] An early example of the use of information of this sort is provided by Gerald Manners, 'Some Costs of Urban Growth: Implications for South East Wales', *Town and Country Planning,* February 1965. This article discussed the most suitable way of dealing with the expansion problem of the Cardiff region and recommended that the balance of advantage could lie in the creation of a new town of 160,000-170,000 population.

[4] The most frequently quoted study of this issue is by K. S. Lomax, 'The Relationship Between Expenditure per Head and Size of Population of County Boroughs in England and Wales', *Journal of the Royal Statistical Society,* Vol. 106, No. 2, 1943. On the basis of pre-war data Professor Lomax was able to show that the costs of providing education, libraries, parks and other rate-financed services were probably at a minimum at population levels of 100,000-150,000. The work has not, apparently, been updated. Readers interested in methodology may consult G. M. Neutze, *Economic Policy and the Size of Cities,* Australian National University Press, Canberra, 1966.

and foster improved social and community services (benefits), though perhaps at the expense of reduced access to countryside or increased transport difficulties (disbenefits). Immediately we are forced back to listing a range of features which do not lend themselves easily to monetary evaluation.

D. Regional Planning

Regional planning problems have not so far been tackled rigorously in terms of cost-benefit analysis. The inherent difficulties can best be illustrated by considering an outline exercise in drawing up a purely qualitative advantages-disadvantages balance sheet by Mr L. C. Kitching as an aid to solving the problems of South-East England.[1] Given an expected population increase in the area of some 2-4 million persons by 1980, five possibilities for providing accommodation were considered:

1. unrestricted growth of the conurbation;

2. intensification of the development plans for growth in towns close to London;

3. concentration of growth in one new city;

4. concentration in 6 to 12 new cities planned for an initial quarter of a million population and sited well away from London; or

5. the development of linear towns stretching outward from London.

Part of the advantages of each possibility centre on the extent to which congestion and other social costs within London would be relieved. Measurement would be formidably difficult. As we have seen, some of the problems which might arise in transport have been approached, but many of the other advantages and disadvantages are more or less immeasurable. Unrestricted growth would certainly increase the problems of an increasingly unhealthy environment, make the provision of open space and recreational facilities harder, and possibly deplete the economy of the remainder of the country. Growth in towns near London or linear extensions might reduce congestion in the conurbation less than would other schemes. Six to twelve new cities would spread the economic benefits over a wider area.

At this stage it is sufficient to say that regional planning teams have not sought to bring all the relevant factors in devising regional planning strategies into relationship with the measuring rod of money. A planning strategy, by its nature, is multi-dimensional and, to use the words of the South-East Joint Planning Team:

[1] L. C. Kitching, 'Conurbation into City Region—How should London Grow?', *Journal of the Town Planning Institute*, November 1963.

'there are no agreed techniques for testing objectively the costs and effectiveness of inter-related policies (e.g., on industrial location, transport and housing)'.[1] We return to this issue at the conclusion of the next section.

E. THE THIRD LONDON AIRPORT

The Government's appointment of a Commission

'to inquire into the timing of the need for a four-runway airport to cater for the growth of traffic at existing airports serving the London area, to consider the various alternative sites and to recommend which site should be selected'

was announced in February 1968. A final report, prepared under the chairmanship of Mr Justice Roskill, which recommended that the airport be constructed at Cublington in Buckinghamshire, was completed in December 1970 and published in January 1971.[2] Subsequently the Government concluded that the Commission's advice should be disregarded and plans are now in preparation for development on a coastal site at Foulness, in Essex.[3] The Commission adopted a form of cost-benefit analysis as an aid to decision-making and a research team was asked to quantify the costs if the airport were constructed at four 'short-listed' sites—Cublington, Foulness, Thurleigh (Bedfordshire), and Nuthampstead (Hertfordshire)—selected from an initial list of 78 'possibles'.

The Roskill Report is not easy to understand. A description of many important steps in the analysis can be found only from close reading of the Final Report, its appendices, and the technical reports. The whole exercise was based on detailed forecasts of air traffic movement for up to 30 years, and it included a large number of technical and scientific investigations. It was this underlying work which formed the input for the cost-benefit analysis. The results are subject to margins of error arising from the obvious and inevitable technical and economic uncertainties in any long-period study.

[1] South-East Joint Planning Team, *op. cit.*, p. 167. This statement does not mean that regional planners adopt a wholly eclectic approach. Efforts are being made to evolve methods of appraisal, notably the 'goals achievement matrix' technique, which allow for the measurement, by scales of effectiveness, of the advantages and disadvantages of various spatial forms of development as methods of achieving a range of planning objectives. This technique, which has much in common with the use of the 'Planning Balance Sheet' in analysing urban development schemes, helps to focus attention on relevant factors, though it involves a high degree of subjective judgement in measuring 'effectiveness' and even more difficulties in attaching 'weights' to each objective. The 'weighted scores', arrived at by combining scale measurement with weights, become the basis for choice. An example is examined in Notts-Derby Sub-Regional Planning Unit, *Notts-Derby Sub-Regional Plan*, HMSO, 1969.

[2] Commission on the Third London Airport, *op. cit.* Nine other voluminous sets of papers and proceedings have been published of which Vol. VII contains the details of the cost-benefit analysis. A summary account, prepared by a member of the research staff, is easily available in A. D. J. Flowerdew, 'Choosing a Site for the Third London Airport: The Roskill Commission's Approach', in R. Layard (ed.), *Cost-Benefit Analysis, Selected Readings*, Penguin Modern Economics Readings, Penguin Books, 1972.

[3] The site is now referred to as 'Maplin'.

The cost-benefit analysis will be described selectively with the minimum of comment. Attention will then be turned to the issues raised in the heated debate aroused by the Commission's work.[1]

The Cost-Benefit Analysis

The easiest way of approaching the subject is to refer to the Commission's terms of reference and to clarify the fundamentals of the Roskill approach. A commercial investment appraisal involves the comparison of costs with revenue with the ultimate objective of deriving a rate of return on capital. If there are externalities the private return may, in certain circumstances, be modified to convert the result into a social rate of return. An airport can be regarded as a commercial investment—it has capital and running costs and it obtains revenues from landing fees and from the other commercial services—but it produces external disbenefits, particularly noise nuisance. As an aid to planning the Government could have asked for a comparative estimate of the social rate of return to airport investment, but did not. The fundamental assumption, instead, was that the 'need' for a third airport was firmly established and that, leaving aside timing problems (the investigation of which was a relatively minor part of the Commission's work), all that had to be decided was location. The task then resolved itself into the detailed costing of airport provision at each potential site and the choice of the cheapest alternative. Methodologically the process can best be described as a 'cost-effectiveness' study. For this reason the results in Table III[2] are shown in terms of costs and do not directly mention benefits.[3]

A number of cost items raised no large valuation problems. These include items (i) airport construction costs (note that the resource costs absorbed by Foulness are shown to be £30 million higher than those estimated for Cublington, and £52 million higher than the Thurleigh figure), (ii) costs of provision of airport services[4] (water, sewage, electricity, etc.), (vii) defence costs (associated mainly with moving various

[1] A sample of this literature would include: E. J. Mishan, 'What is Wrong with Roskill?', *Journal of Transport Economics and Policy*, Vol. 4, No. 3, 1970, reprinted in Layard, *op. cit.*; N. Lichfield, 'Cost-Benefit Analysis in Planning; A Critique of the Roskill Commission', *Regional Studies*, Vol. 5, No. 3, 1971; and D. W. Pearce, *Cost-Benefit Analysis*, Macmillan, London, 1971. The same issue of *Regional Studies* contains articles by J. Parry-Lewis, R. C. Carruthers and H. M. Dale, and F. H. Sharman, which deal with traffic forecasting. Interesting views are set out by P. Self, *op. cit.*, and by Professor Sir Colin Buchanan in his 'Note of Dissent' to the Report.

[2] The Table is not presented in the form favoured by the Commission. Their well-known summary (*Report*, Table 12.1, p. 119) shows differences, for each of the 20 factors, from the costs applicable to the least-cost site, plus the aggregate of inter-site differences. Though the latter became the basis for choice the underlying estimates place the various items in perspective. The discount factor was 10 per cent and 1982 was taken as the 'base year' on the ground that the airport would then be operational.

[3] An important qualification of this statement relevant to user costs is indicated below, p. 52.

[4] This item does, in fact, include some time valuations relating to so-called 'taxing costs'. For simplicity we will not discuss the item in detail here. The reader will appreciate that we cannot do more in a short study than bring out some of the major points which, if his interest is aroused, can be followed up in detail in the Report and elsewhere.

military establishments), and (vi) the capital necessary for road and rail links. Item (ix) 'other costs' covers a heterogeneous bunch of factors (the minutiae included the much-debated value of Stewkley Church), and we have already discussed (iii) the valuation of agricultural land (above, pp. 39-41). We are left with (iv) airspace movement costs, (v) user costs, and (viii) noise.

Movement and user- cost problems

The first two are critically affected by alternative assumptions relating to the value of time and by the accuracy of the forecasts of airport use. Airspace movement costs (item (iv) in Table III) vary partly because the alternative sites were expected to attract different amounts of utilisation, but also because flying time between the airport and the start of the major air lanes at the edges of the London air traffic

TABLE III

The Third London Airport: Cost-Benefit Analysis of Four 'Short-listed' Sites[1]

	Cublington		*Foulness*		*Nuthampst'd*		*Thurleigh*	
	(£ million discounted to 1982)							
i. Airport construction[2]	303		335		300		283	
ii. Airport services	127	(113)	104	(91)	121	(108)	111	(98)
iii. Agriculture	8		11		16		10	
iv. Airspace movement costs	1,899	(1,685)	1,906	(1,690)	1,934	(1,716)	1,929	(1,711)
v. User costs	2,903	(1,763)	3,124	(1,944)	2,949	(1,803)	2,942	(1,785)
vi. Road and rail capital	39		67		52		41	
vii. Defence	73		44		49		105	
viii. Noise	23		21		72		16	
ix. Other costs[3]	58		18		77		84	
Total costs	5,433	(4,065)	5,630	(4,221)	5,570	(4,193)	5,521	(4,133)
Aggregate of inter-site differences	*0*		*197*	*(156)*	*137*	*(128)*	*88*	*(68)*

[1] *Source:* Roskill Commission *Report, op. cit.,* Appendix 20; Table 12.1 for the aggregate of inter-site differences, and other detailed tables for the details under each head. Bracketed figures are based on 'low' time values (below, p. 52). All annual values were discounted at 10 per cent.

[2] Including Luton extensions. In the case of Foulness these would cost £20 million compared with £2·5 million for each of the other sites.

[3] Meteorology, air safety, scientific establishments, private airfields, on-site residential conditions, public buildings, commerce and industry, recreation.

51

control sector would differ depending upon airport location (aircraft using the North Atlantic route, for example, would travel further to reach Foulness than Cublington). The costs measured therefore include those of aircraft operation and travellers' time. Similarly user costs include rail fares or road transport costs plus time valuations, the number of passengers[1] affected again varying with airport location.

Here there is a snag. The traffic forecasts indicated that by 2000 Foulness usage would be some 7 per cent lower than at Cublington, and also less than at the other two sites; in short there is a relationship between accessibility and traffic flows. Since cost differences are the key to the final recommendation it would be wrong to ignore this factor—implicitly one would tilt the balance in favour of the least accessible site! A way therefore had to be found for crediting all sites other than Foulness with a value reflecting their more convenient situation. The calculations were complex since they involved the manipulation of a 'gravity model' for forecasting traffic flows, which would indicate the extra trips generated by the choice of any of the inland sites. As in other transport studies[2] the value placed on such 'generated traffic' was recorded at one-half of the time- and cost-savings advantage of the inland site compared with Foulness. Hence the figures shown for Cublington, Nuthampstead and Thurleigh are the basic user costs *minus* the imputed advantages accruing to them because of their locational superiority for airport users.

Since airport user costs and airspace movement costs ((v) and (iv) in Table III) assume such large importance in the whole exercise, their valuation is of vital significance. And since cost differences emerge as residuals, they can be critically affected by changes in the underlying aggregates.[3] Furthermore, since both items include time valuations, the latter must be carefully examined. The original research study split travellers into 'business' and 'leisure', valuing time for the former at the average hourly cost of employment (£2·32). Leisure passengers' time values were placed at 23 pence and 5 pence per hour for adults and children respectively. These figures were for 1968 and were estimated to grow by approximately 3 per cent per annum to reach hourly values of £3·60 for businessmen and 41 pence and 14 pence for adults and children.[4] Realising that time values are questionable, the Commission decided to use 'high' and 'low' figures in their final report. For businessmen they were £2·58

---

[1] Our user-cost figures relate both to passengers and freight. Again, for simplicity we can ignore the latter.

[2] Above, p. 30.

[3] For example, in national income accounting any item estimated as a residual difference between large totals can vary widely in percentage terms if there is a *small* percentage change in either aggregate —the estimate of personal savings is an excellent example.

[4] Leisure time here is valued on Department of the Environment standards which now regard time as worth 25 per cent of the hourly wage-earnings of travellers—the 3 per cent factor accounts for growth in living standards. No real justification is provided for applying these values to nonworking members of the travelling public, and the allowance for children remained virtually unexplained.

and £1·46 per hour; for leisure time the values were 50 per cent above and below those employed in the research study.

Valuation of noise

In considering valuation we must turn, finally, to problems of noise. For comparative purposes it is interesting to note that some 700,000 households are within the noise 'shadow' of Heathrow.[1] Estimates of those likely to be similarly afflicted by the third airport were 95,000 for Nuthampstead, and 20,000-30,000 for the alternative sites. The valuation procedure was extremely complex. Householders affected by a build-up of noise can either remain and suffer worsening living conditions, or move and suffer property depreciation (including removal costs) and the loss of 'householders' surplus'. The former was estimated by a survey of the property market in the Gatwick airport area which showed that there is a relationship between noise intensity and house prices.[2] The concept of 'householders' surplus' simply refers to the amount of money over and above the market price of property which owners would require to induce them to make a willing sale: it reflects such factors as personal ties to a house, locality or circle of friends. From a survey in areas unlikely to be affected by noise the average value of householders' surplus was placed at 39 per cent above market values, though attempts were made to recognise that the precise figure can vary between householders. There are two obvious problems at this stage: forecasting the number of households likely to move, whose 'loss' could be estimated by the method just described, and ascribing a noise nuisance value to non-movers. Here previous evidence, based on psycho-sociological survey material, yielded a frequency distribution, for each noise and nuisance index (NNI) value, showing the proportion of persons within the population who expressed varying degrees of annoyance from aircraft disturbance (some, apparently, are 'imperturbable'). The annoyance scores taken as an index were then translated into monetary values by assuming that the median score could be equated with the average property depreciation in the Gatwick area at the appropriate NNI level. This procedure may appear completely outlandish—until it is remembered that 'depreciated' property is sold on the market, and the 'discount' revealed is presumably related to the purchaser's subjective valuation of the disamenity of noise.[3] Given this information, movement is

[1] Noise levels are measured by a 'noise and nuisance index' (NNI) which is a weighted average of noise intensity and frequency. People 'affected' are taken as members of households within the 35 NNI contour—in the event of an airport being built many more people would be disturbed to a lesser degree.

[2] Percentage rates of depreciation rose to 29 per cent for the most expensive class of property in the noisiest areas and to about 10 per cent for the cheapest homes.

[3] The *Report*, Appendix 22, contains a long account of other possible assumptions. For example, purchasers of 'noisy' property could well be persons whose 'noise annoyance' score is below the median (i.e., the more 'imperturbable'). Use of the 'lower quartile' as the equating point would raise noise costs by about 50 per cent.

forecast by estimating the number of households for whom noise nuisance values are likely to be *larger than* the sum of depreciation and householders' surplus, the latter two items being taken as their total noise loss. The non-movers are then allotted a nuisance cost depending on the translation of the annoyance level scores into money values, as described above.[1]

The Roskill Commission: Appraisal

One misunderstanding can be disposed of immediately. There is apparently a widespread impression (fostered partly by Professor Colin Buchanan's 'Note of Dissent') that the Commission were prepared to recommend the choice of the lowest-cost site regardless of all other considerations. Certainly no estimates were made of the environmental worth of the Cublington site, nor of the ecological and recreational value of Maplin sands. Nor did the Commission place a value on the possibility of a Foulness development triggering off 'a regenerative process reaching right back into the heart of London where the East End butts against the City'.[2] There is no way in which such valuations could be made. But a reading of Chapter 6, on land-use planning, should be enough to convince anyone that the Commission were alive to the possibility that costs alone, as identified in the analysis, should be viewed as only one piece of relevant evidence. Put simply, their argument was that the lowest-cost site did not have other disadvantages associated with it which would made it unacceptable, and that the Foulness development would not foster the achievement of wider planning goals to make its cost disadvantage unimportant. The Government has taken a different view—it is a question of 'trading off' a cost difference against qualitative political and environmental factors. Since this decision must involve value-judgements, debate can become futile.

It could be argued, however, that the Commission were somewhat over-assertive in emphasising the costed inferiority of the Foulness site, which they placed at £156-£199 million. The estimates were based on an inherently difficult long-period traffic forecast and some valuations are also open to suspicion (below, p. 55). In terms of identified costs Foulness was shown to be some 3·6 or 3·8 per cent more

---

[1] The method can be summarised easily in symbols. For each NNI level a frequency distribution is formed of annoyance scores, the median of the distribution being taken as equal to the corresponding estimate of property depreciation (D). The result is a distribution of imputed values of noise annoyance (N) among households within the zone involved. If S is the value of householders' surplus a household is expected to move if $N > S + D$. Here $S + D$ is taken as the loss involved. Conversely, if $N < S + D$ the household is expected to stay in the noise-affected zone. Here N is taken as the appropriate loss.

[2] 'Note of Dissent', *Report*, p. 158. Professor Buchanan's view was that the eastern side of London is an economically and socially disadvantaged area, particularly in comparison with the west, and that a regenerative effect could arise if a major new source of employment became available. The locational advantages of the area would presumably also be strengthened to some degree.

expensive than Cublington—a very narrow margin when all the uncertainties and difficulties are considered.[1]

Valuation controversy

Two costing items attracted particular controversy. The first, not unexpectedly, concerns the treatment of travelling time. It was in this item that the inferiority of Foulness became particularly marked. The point is familiar enough—can leisure time (often short for each individual) be valued by reference to earnings? Is housewives' and children's time saving amenable to any sensible treatment? Does a businessman's delay inflict severe opportunity costs on the nation as a whole? The Commission argued that time *is* important and they stuck to the basic logic of their approach. What they failed to point out was that their calculations rested on a flimsy basis.[2] As Dr Mishan has observed, there is 'clearly some margin to be got by playing around with such figures, and this makes any choice on economic grounds alone appear somewhat less satisfactory'.[3]

On the question of noise two aspects of the Commission's procedure can be questioned. First, the estimation of 'householders' surplus' was obtained from a sample survey conducted in areas unlikely to be affected by airport noise—indeed persons were asked to imagine their reactions to a situation in which their homes were wanted 'to form part of a large development scheme' and that a developer was making an offer to purchase. Though a sum above market price necessary to compensate for the loss of 'householders' surplus' can be derived in this way, the natural reaction of people questioned would very possibly be to assume that they could move a *short* distance away and suffer little or no dislocation of their social and working lives. The resulting figures do not necessarily indicate the amount necessary to compensate them if their whole locality is invaded by noise from which they cannot escape without *major* disruption.

Secondly, an extremely high discount rate (10 per cent) was used to convert estimates of the growth of noise nuisance to present-value terms. This rate reduces any valuation for a period of more than 20 years to very small discounted sums.[4]

Finally, we must raise a basic principle. The Commission was required, fundamentally, to do little more than make a choice of site for a third airport. They were

---

[1] Note that the research team's analysis set out costs in the general form shown in Table III. The *Report* focussed attention on inter-site differences—the totals, it was said (*Report,* p. 118), have no relevance. This is true, but the research team seemed far more ready than the Commission to admit of possible error, and to inquire assiduously into the sensitivity of the results.

[2] The research team's work showed that the removal of leisure-time savings from the calculation, and the reduction of the value of business time by 25 per cent from £2·32 per hour made Thurleigh the least-cost site. Cublington's advantage over Foulness was reduced to £32 million.

[3] Mishan, *op. cit.*

[4] The rate of discount of 10 per cent was based on the general criteria, evolved from a consideration of the opportunity cost of capital, now (1973) employed in appraising public sector investment. One could again argue that so high a rate is inappropriate as a basis for social appraisal.

not expected to demonstrate that the airport would prove to be a commercially viable proposition. More importantly, they were not asked to show that its viability could be preserved if airport and airline operators were faced with paying charges related, in some way, to the noise nuisance of air transport.[1] Valuation still presents difficulties and the size of an appropriate charge would be difficult to determine. Nevertheless the economist must ask whether air travel, given that fare levels do not reflect nuisance, is not under-priced, with consequent effects on demand. Had the Commission been invited to begin with a broader-ranging study of *pricing* problems, and on this basis to inquire further into airport demand rather than 'needs', the final results and recommendations might have been more satisfactory in reflecting public preferences between different locations and between air travel and other expenditures.

---

[1] This point was made forcibly in the research team's study where it was said that 'it is not enough to state that an investment can be justified purely by the public demand for the services it provides. It must also be demonstrated that the demand is sufficiently strong to outweigh all costs and disbenefits which are incurred, particularly if some of those are not directly met by air traffic revenue'. (Commission on the Third London Airport, *Papers and Proceedings,* Vol. VII, HMSO, London, 1970,p. 103.) Unfortunately the issue was not rigorously debated.

V Other Applications

This Section considers six further applications of cost-benefit analysis: military defence, health services, education, recreational provision, port investment, and research and development. It also comments briefly on aspects of nationalised industry policy.

1. Military defence

Military defence is a 'collective good' of the most fundamental type. It would be stretching terminology to the limit to conceive of a 'rate of return' to investment in defence comparable to rates of return obtainable in other forms of investment. Most of the work on this subject is therefore concerned with 'cost-of-effectiveness' studies dealing with such issues as the relative potency of weapon systems in relation to costs, the cost of reducing risks to shipping, or of alternative defensive arrangements.[1] Given the enormous call of defence expenditure on national resources, the aim is to maximise the impact of the available funds and to seek means whereby economies may be achieved without loss of efficiency.

In the United States military operational research of this nature has become a highly developed science and a number of specialised agencies devote time and resources to it. The proposal that similar cost-effectiveness work should be undertaken in Britain was made in the 1965 Defence White Paper[2] and a similar specialist study unit charged with inquiring into problems raised in the three armed services was created in Britain.

The efficient allocation of scarce military resources raises many familiar cost-benefit problems. Externalities develop when the actions of one arm of the service affect the ease with which tasks may be performed elsewhere. Tactical weapons, originally designed to support troops on the ground, can add to strategic potentialities. Siting a base close to large urban areas can, by increasing the likelihood of attack, add to the difficulties of civil defence.

Another familiar difficulty arises out of possible confusion in the interpretation of cost-benefit ratios. Suppose 'benefits' are measured by a scale of effectiveness in destroying targets, and costs in monetary terms. A low-cost, low-effectiveness weapon system, for instance a bomber force, nevertheless has a high ratio of 'benefit' to 'cost'. As Professor Roland N. McKean writes, 'it may be a way of doing almost nothing

---

[1] Discussions of the techniques are in C. J. Hitch and R. N. McKean, *Economics of Defence in the Nuclear Age,* OUP, 1961, and in an article by McKean in A. T. Peacock and D. J. Robertson (eds.), *Public Expenditure—Appraisal and Control,* Oliver & Boyd, 1963.
[2] *Statement on the Defence Estimates,* Cmnd. 2592, HMSO, 1965.

but doing it particularly well'. The solution is to conduct the analysis in terms of increments in effectiveness compared with increments in costs. Finally, as a last example, the problem of 'capital intensity' is also common: how is a choice to be made between the high initial costs combined with low subsequent costs and the reverse?

2. Health expenditure

Some work, notably in the United States, has been attempted on the economics of expenditure on health.[1] Two approaches are common. In the first place 'global' analyses attempt to identify the benefits from health expenditure in general. At first sight the costs may appear easily identifiable; after all, the requisites must be purchased in the market. But health depends not only upon the amounts of medical services but also upon a host of other factors such as the standard of housing and general cleanliness, and the level of diet. Separation of the two is virtually impossible. Similar difficulties arise when the 'yield' is being estimated.

The normal approach is to attempt valuations based on the concept of production foregone as the result of illness. If the working time lost as a result of health programmes can be estimated, it must be valued as a time stream and appropriately discounted—an enormously complicated task. If average earnings are used as the yardstick there is the immediate difficulty of deciding how future unemployment is to be included in the calculation, and of projecting a time stream which is affected by underlying rates of economic growth. Growth implies that anyone whose life is saved 'today' can look forward to a gradually rising stream of future earnings. But there is an obvious danger in ascribing to health expenditure a benefit which in reality cannot be dissociated from benefits from additional education, technological innovation or any other determinant of the rate of economic growth.

Exactly similar problems arise in less ambitious analyses of types of health expenditure. Professor Burton Weisbrod prepared tentative estimates of the costs to society of various diseases, mainly in an effort to suggest means by which medical research might be best directed.[2] Others have given money values to the benefits associated with attempts to check the spread of contagious infections. In another study Mr R. W. Conley examined the economic advantages associated with the vocational rehabilitation of the mentally and physically disabled.[3] He demonstrated convincingly that in many cases such programmes are financially feasible because the potential gains in output exceed the cost of rehabilitation to the taxpayer, even allowing for additional costs on employers of disabled persons. Mr Conley admitted

[1] S. J. Mushkin, 'Health as an Investment', *Journal of Political Economy*, October 1962 (Supplement).
[2] Burton A. Weisbrod, *Economics of Public Health*, Pennsylvania University Press, 1962.
[3] R. W. Conley, *The Economics of Vocational Rehabilitation*, Johns Hopkins University Press and Oxford University Press, 1965. In Britain family planning services have been appraised by W. Laing, *The Costs and Benefits of Family Planning*, Broadsheet No. 534, Political and Economic Planning, London, 1972.

that the wider benefits of such programmes to the disabled and their relatives were exceedingly difficult to quantify.

There are other difficulties. Productive time saved is the most easily recognisable benefit which can be quantified, but the incidence of diseases is not uniform between the sexes, which immediately raises one of the oldest and most intractable problems of economic measurement—the assessment of the value of housewives' services. In the end the whole approach also tends to collapse because improved health has a 'consumption' aspect: illness impairs both the sufferer's earning power (if an earner) and capacity to enjoy life. Plainly also disease incidence is not uniform between age groups. What is the economic value of the life of a retired person or of an infant? This problem boils down to valuing life itself, a task which clearly cannot—and, many would say, should not—be undertaken by the economist, except in the most arbitrary way.

In Britain most economic analysis of health service expenditure has concentrated on the operational aspects of running a vast and complex service.[1] Amongst the techniques of interest in this *Paper* the 'cost-of-effectiveness' approach appears to be dominant.[2] The basic aim is to isolate the costs associated with types of care and to seek means of encouraging operational efficiency. Yet many of the problems of the health service stem from the difficulties of allocating sufficient sums to it ('sufficient' being a social value-judgement), and of providing choice between quantities and qualities of treatment. Here cost-benefit analysis appears to be of little direct relevance.[3]

The costs of road accidents

Another related matter which has aroused interest in Britain concerns the problem of assessing the 'costs' of road accidents. The major work is that of Mr R. F. F. Dawson[4] who attempted an updating and refinement of the earlier studies of Mr D. J. Reynolds and others.[5] The measurable cost to the community of road accidents in Britain in 1965 was placed at £246 million, the 'health element' (loss of future output

[1] For a critical assessment of the NHS, Professor John and Mrs Sylvia Jewkes, *The Genesis of the British National Health Service*, Blackwell, 1961, *Value for Money in Medicine*, Blackwell, 1963, and 'Britain out of Step', in *Monopoly or Choice in Health Services?*, Occasional Paper 3, IEA, 1964.
[2] For further discussion, Professor Jack Wiseman, 'Cost-Benefit Analysis and Health Service Policy', in Peacock and Robertson, *op. cit.*, and M. S. Feldstein, 'Economic Analysis, Operational Research and the National Health Service', *Oxford Economic Papers*, March 1963. In his paper Professor Wiseman added the cryptic comment: 'If growth is the sole aim of the policy maker there might be a strong case for providing only one medical service for the aged: euthanasia'.
[3] Aspects of this issue are debated in Professor D. S. Lees, *Health through Choice*, Hobart Paper 14, IEA, 1961, reprinted in *Freedom or Free-for-All?*, IEA, 1965, and J. M. Buchanan, *The Inconsistencies of the National Health Service*, Occasional Paper 7, IEA, 1965.
[4] *Cost of Road Accidents in Great Britain*, RRL Report LR79, Road Research Laboratory, Crowthorne, 1967.
[5] D. J. Reynolds, 'The Cost of Road Accidents', *Journal of the Royal Statistical Society,* Vol. 119, Part 4, 1956.

of those killed or injured, net of the loss of the consumption of those killed) at £24 million. The discounting factor used was 6 per cent in contrast to Reynolds's 4 per cent. The calculation extended to medical treatment (£12 million), damage to property (£164 million), and administrative expenses by police and insurance companies (£28 million). The average cost per accident involving personal injury or death was placed at £360 though Mr Dawson was quick to argue that this figure should in principle be raised to include the 'subjective costs' of bereavement and suffering associated with accidents. He argued that the *economic* cost to the community (£246 million) was less than the community would be willing to pay to reduce accidents. On the basis of purely arbitrary valuations of £5,000 per fatal accident and £200 per serious injury, the average cost per accident was estimated at £560. It was suggested that this sort of figure could be used in assessing the effectiveness, in relation to cost, of accident reduction.[1]

A discussion of the shadow-pricing technique best suited to measuring the benefits of programmes affecting risk of mortality was provided by Professor T. C. Schelling who was very critical of approaches which relied only on measurement of potential effects on output minus the loss of the deceased's consumption.[2] He argued that a reduction in the risk of death was best evaluated in terms of the amount the affected individuals would be willing to pay themselves. In short, is there a direct market indicator which could be used as a basis for imputation? This subject is exceedingly difficult. An obvious choice is insurance information though the aim is not to place a subjective valuation on life as such but to protect dependants. Court decisions on damages are often based on similar considerations. Professor Schelling suggested market research interview techniques, though they would produce results dependent to a large extent on the incomes of the sample.

3. *The rate of return to education*

Many would confess to a distaste for considering health expenditure in cold economic terms. But 'investment in human capital' in education provokes fewer inhibitions. One of the most interesting current economic debates concerns the means of accelerating rates of growth in national product. It used to be widely held that the surest way lay in increasing the rate of capital formation. Recent studies which have attempted to account for growth in terms of the increasing supplies of labour and capital have concluded that alone they do not account for all recorded changes; a 'residual' element is normally attributed to increases in knowledge and skills.[3] As a result more expenditure on education is frequently held desirable. If, so the argument

[1] For an application, R. E. Allsop, *Costs and Benefits Arising if All Motorcyclists Wore Crash Helmets,* RRL Report LR72, Road Research Laboratory, Crowthorne, 1967.
[2] T. C. Schelling, 'The Life You Save May be Your Own', in Samuel B. Chase, *Problems in Public Expenditure Analysis,* The Brookings Institution, Washington DC, 1968.
[3] Colin Clark, *Growthmanship*, Hobart Paper 10, reprinted in *Ancient or Modern?*, IEA, 1965.

runs, the return to educational investment could be measured it is likely to be such as to indicate the desirability of increasing expenditures for purely economic reasons. The benefits of education are likely to accrue primarily to individuals through increases in potential earning power, but there are also 'external benefits'.[1] Some, such as the increases in productive power of society as a whole through the growth of specialist skills and organisational ability, are in principle measurable in economic terms. Others are far less tangible. Presumably future generations gain as a result of the educational level of the parent generation; an educational system will afford a means of organising and developing exceptional talent; it will ensure more flexibility in the occupational distribution of the labour force; it may promote respect for law and order and increase political stability; it will widen the scope for enjoyment of leisure.[2] Since it would be impossible to argue the case for and against these propositions exclusively in terms of their economic value, most work on the rates of return to education concentrates on the more quantifiable variables, generally attempting to assess the gains in earning power from education to varying stages along with some effort to encompass the economic spill-overs.

Difficulty of calculating rates of return

Though there is no general agreement on terminology, we may regard the private rate of return to education as the relationship between privately appropriated gains (additional income less tax) minus private costs (primarily income foregone during the period of education plus fees).[3] The social return is arrived at by comparing additional income (before tax) plus any economic spill-overs which can be identified, with the full social costs (income foregone, private fees, and state aid).

The major difficulty in such calculations is that of distinguishing the effects of education upon earning power from other factors. Earnings may also be related to social class and to individuals' basic intelligence and drive. Furthermore, in a sample survey to collect information means must be found of assessing income levels through their working lives of persons with different types of education. Inevitably, therefore,

[1] John Vaizey, *The Economics of Education*, Faber and Faber, 1962; Theodor Schultz, *The Economic Value of Education*, Columbia University Press, 1961. A most useful summary of the debate is in Mark Blaug, 'The Rate of Return on Investment in Education in Great Britain', *Manchester School of Economic and Social Studies*, September 1965. This article is reprinted in M. Blaug (ed.), *The Economics of Education 1*, Penguin Modern Economics Readings, Penguin Books, 1968. A second volume of readings appeared in 1969 and there is an extended discussion of cost-benefit analysis in M. Blaug, *An Introduction to the Economics of Education*, Penguin Books, 1970, Ch. 6-8; A. T. Peacock and Jack Wiseman, *Education for Democrats*, Hobart Paper 25, IEA, 1964 (re-issued 1970), deal with aspects of educational policy.
[2] A wide-ranging discussion of these questions is in E. G. West, *Education and the State*, IEA, 1965 (Second Edition with an extended Introduction by the author, 1970).
[3] We are here discussing of course only full-time formal education, though it would be naïve to suppose that all education takes place at institutions of learning. This important qualification is a further complicating factor which few commentators have taken into account: E. G. West, *ibid.*, especially Part II.

61

the effects measured reflect the quality of education received up to 50 years ago. Moreover, relative labour rewards, at any one time, may be poor indicators of future incomes as conditions in the labour market change. Finally, any rate of return calculation, to be significant, must be based on the assumption that workers are paid the value of their marginal product—which may be invalidated because of monopoly influences in the labour market[1] and which can also be affected by such non-pecuniary rewards as the inherent satisfaction of jobs and the sense of vocation which impels people to accept low money rewards. Given these difficulties (not to mention the obvious fact that marriage removes many educated women from the labour market for some period of their lives), it is not surprising that some economists, such as Mr Stephen Merrett, have argued that research into rates of return should be discontinued.[2]

Researchers not deterred

Nevertheless, many examples of research could be quoted. Most come from the United States.[3] In Britain, the first study originated from the National Economic Development Office[4] and was concerned with the advantages of three-year schooling beyond the age of 15. On the basis of a sample survey comparing the incomes of people who left school at 15 and 18, with corrections for social class and other 'background' factors derived from American evidence, the social rate of return was placed tentatively at 12·5 per cent and the private rate at 13 per cent. The exercise could not be adequately duplicated for three additional years of higher education, though the figures were tentatively placed at 6 per cent for the social rate and 20 per cent for the private rate. A later survey, sponsored by the Department of Education and Science, and carried out by Miss Vera Morris and Dr A. Ziderman, was much more ambitious.[5] Using an extensive earnings survey and information relating to detailed costings of various forms and levels of education (they could not be broken down by subject),[6] a range of social (internal) rates of return was calculated.

[1] D. S. Lees, *The Economic Consequences of the Professions,* Research Monograph 2, IEA, 1967.

[2] Stephen Merrett, 'The Rate of Return to Education: A Critique', *Oxford Economic Papers,* November 1966.

[3] G. S. Becker, *Human Capital: A Theoretical and Empirical Analysis with Special Reference to Education,* National Bureau of Economic Research and Columbia University Press, New York, 1965; B. W. Wilkinson, 'Present Values of Lifetime Earnings in Different Occupations', *Journal of Political Economy,* December 1966. In an interesting study of Israel's experience in the period 1951-57 the surprising conclusion was reached that advanced education was yielding little or no social gain. Negative returns to medical and legal studies were only partially offset by positive returns to engineering and accountancy training: R. Klinov-Malul, *The Profitability of Investment in Education in Israel,* Maurice Falk Institute, Jerusalem, 1966.

[4] Prepared by D. Henderson-Stewart and published as an appendix to Professor Blaug's *Manchester School* article, *op. cit.*

[5] V. Morris and A. Ziderman, 'The Economic Return on Investment in Higher Education in England and Wales', *Economic Trends,* HMSO, May 1971, pp. XX-XXXI.

[6] Disaggregated material, relating to returns to technological education in the electrical engineering sector, is provided by P. R. G. Layard *et al., Qualified Manpower and Economic Performance,* Allen Lane, The Penguin Press, 1971.

A selection of the results, arranged in the form of 'incremental comparisons', is shown in Table IV.[1]

TABLE IV
Estimates of Social Rates of Return to Education: Males, 1966-67

	With no ability adjustment %	With ability adjustment %
'A' Level/Non-Qualified	7·6	6·9
ONC/Non-Qualified	7·9	7·0
HNC/ONC	>20·0	>20·0
HNC-PQ/HNC	20·0	16·0
First Degree/A-Level	10·8	9·2
Master's/First Degree	1·2	<0·0
Doctorate/First Degree	1·6	<0·0

Source: Morris & Ziderman, op. cit.

The authors were quick to point out that the results are subject to all the difficulties and uncertainties outlined on pages 61-62.[2] They also make it clear that any guidance which might be obtained from rate-of-return calculations should be regarded as an adjunct to other approaches which seek to throw light on what they describe as the 'unresolved' question of the appropriate scale of provision of higher education.[3] The implications of their results are that the highest social rates of return are obtained from technical qualifications (Ordinary National Certificates, Higher National Certificates, particularly those supplemented to 'professional qualification' level) and from first degrees. The social value (excluding 'external effects') of further education to master's degree or doctorate level is derisory.[4] The results do not mean

[1] The original article presents all the basic earnings and costing information. Our extract relates to returns on costs which include a 'research cost' element.

[2] They are particularly concerned with distinguishing the effects on earnings of 'intrinsic ability' and 'education per se' (Table IV). From American evidence, based on extensive statistical analysis of the determinants of personal incomes, they reduce earnings, and thus lower the rates of return, by a factor of approximately one-third. This is the 'ability adjustment'. For reasons of the kind mentioned in the text the data do not include the incomes of some professional people (doctors, dentists, lawyers, etc.) and also exclude teachers and the clergy.

[3] The Robbins Committee eschewed consideration of a rate-of-return approach to educational planning, basing their calculations of required provision on estimates of the numbers of qualified students presenting themselves for entry—now termed a 'social demand' approach. Further discussion of its relationship to the 'rate of return' and 'manpower planning' methodology is in Blaug, An Introduction to the Economics of Education, op. cit., and 'Approaches to Educational Planning', Economic Journal, June 1967.

[4] The returns to a first degree (9.2 per cent after the ability adjustment) are below the 'trial rate of discount' of 10 per cent proposed for nationalised industry investment (below, p. 68, fn. 4). Perhaps with this comparison in mind, a number of eminent economists have savagely attacked the methodology. Lord Balogh was moved to ask in the House of Lords who had authorised publication in an official government periodical. He remarked that material of this type gives a grossly distorted picture of the social value of higher education: by this he presumably meant the benefits of 'externalities' immeasurable in monetary terms. At an educational conference in 1972 Dr C. F. Carter (Vice-Chancellor of Lancaster University) remarked that emphasis on economic returns led to a 'battery hen' approach to educational planning.

that a Ph.D. can expect to earn no more than a mere Bachelor; nor do they indicate the *private* advantages of education which, on the basis of Mr Henderson-Stewart's calculations, may be considerable.

Finally, the argument that 'education' should be viewed as an investment (i.e. that it is growth promoting) is likely to be quickly contradicted by the counter-argument that higher education, in particular, has a 'consumption' effect. It is supposedly enjoyable in itself and is a vehicle for widening one's personal horizons regardless of one's subject or future income. Perhaps it is not inappropriate, particularly in an IEA publication, to propose that the strength of demand for these benefits of education might best be tested by some appeal to market forces.

4. Recreation

Given the current interest in the environment it is not surprising that attempts should be made to place values on sites for outdoor recreation. Again, there has been a considerable amount of work on this question in the USA, while more recently British writers have begun to tackle similar issues. The earliest efforts were those of Mr T. L. Burton and Professor G. P. Wibberley[1] who viewed the problem as one of provision of open space near large centres of population which people might use for recreation free of the restrictions that normally operate when land is farmed. Though the authors contend that the decision to provide 'capital-intensive' facilities (swimming baths, bowling alleys, golf courses, etc.) presents few problems, the question arises whether the demand for open space, and the values it generates, is sufficient to justify making it available at the cost of abandoning agriculture and compensating farmers. The problem is regarded, perhaps too simply, as whether or not to provide a public good. It is arbitrarily assumed that any system of charging is likely to prove inoperable.[2]

Valuation faces two difficulties: how can the use of what is essentially a 'non-urban' park be predicted and how can money measures of benefit be obtained? The first requires market research methods to measure annual use likely to be generated from populations situated at varying distances from the recreational area.[3] In their studies of three areas (the Black Mountains in Wales, a Fenland site, and the Ashdown Forest in Kent), Burton and Wibberley used a method of valuation which involved the aggregation of *all* travel costs incurred by recreational visitors. On this basis

[1] *Outdoor Recreation in the British Countryside,* Studies in Rural Land Use No. 5, Wye College, 1965, and further reports in the same series.

[2] Use of a non-urban park is perfectly amenable to the principle of exclusion: a price could be charged. Burton and Wibberley appear to hold that recreation *should* be 'free', which is question-begging; they do not consider pricing solutions. N. W. Mansfield, 'Traffic Policy in the Lake District National Parks', *Journal of Town Planning Institute,* November 1968, reviews the possibilities and suggests road pricing.

[3] It has also been shown that 'gravity models' of trip generation can provide good approximations to observed consumer behaviour. Details are in Peters, *op. cit.,* and N. W. Mansfield, 'The estimation of benefits from recreational sites and the provision of a new recreational facility', *Regional Studies,* July 1971.

64

they concluded that only in one area (Ashdown Forest) were recreational benefits, per annum, larger than agricultural rental values.[1] Though this basis of valuation has frequently been used there is a more ingenious, and conceptually somewhat firmer, approach devised originally by Professor H. Hotelling.[2] It is based on travel costs from various distances converted to obtain a rough measurement of consumers' surplus. The 'marginal consumer', travelling from the furthest distance, is deemed to obtain no surplus.[3] Those who travel shorter distances are then assumed to obtain a surplus measured by the difference between their lower travel costs and those of marginal consumers.

The snag here is that it assumes equal consumer surpluses per visit, regardless of the number of visits. Elementary notions in demand theory suggest that an individual will push his consumption of recreational trips to the point where marginal utility (which presumably declines with the number of trips per unit of time) is equal to 'cost'. Thus the marginal visit provides zero consumer surplus, and the task resolves itself into the much more intricate one of estimating surpluses only on intra-marginal visits. Professor M. Clawson has suggested that this can be done in the following way.[4] Basic data on visits usually allow a relationship to be established between visit *rates* (which tend to decline with distance) and the costs of reaching the recreational site. An answer is then sought to the question: how much use would be made of the recreational area if a hypothetical admission fee, of variable amount, were charged? In theory it is necessary only to assume a range of charges and to calculate from the data the drop in visit *rates* associated with each charge. The charges could then be used as the ordinates of a conventional demand schedule and the total number of visits made at each charge plotted.[5] Consumer surplus is then given as the area under the demand curve as limited by the total number of visits.

Apart from straining the available data to the limit, the method appears appropriate to estimate the value of an *existing* site for which visit data can be obtained.[6] If the likely value of a *new* recreational zone is being estimated (say, a lake created by the construction of a barrage such as those proposed for Morecambe Bay or the Dee estuary), a *forecast* of usage rates must be made—and this, in turn, requires the

[1] The problem can also be seen as involving the valuation of recreational facilities arising as part of a multi-purpose development scheme (above, pp. 25-26).

[2] A. H. Trice and E. E. Wood, 'Measurement of Recreation Benefits', *Land Economics, August 1958*.

[3] For obvious reasons of convenience the margin might be defined as the distance within which, say, 75 per cent of journeys to the area originate. The implicit assumption, of course, is that the drive itself is regarded as a cost whereas one might argue that it, too, should contribute to benefits.

[4] M. Clawson and J. Knetsch, *Economics of Outdoor Recreation,* Resources for the Future, Washington DC, 1968.

[5] As the basic data is normally of visit rates from various 'distance zones' of which the total population is known, it is easy to translate data on *rates* into estimates of *total* visits.

[6] Mansfield (1971), *op. cit.,* attempted to place a 'value' on the Lake District as a recreational zone, arriving at consumer surplus values, by a method similar to Clawson's, of £4,876 per average day for day visits and £27,700 per average week for holiday-makers.

capacity to handle complex problems of a general equilibrium nature. The point, simply, is that visitors would redistribute their trips between existing and new areas, while additional total demand could also be generated. Estimation of these changes, which would in turn affect total consumers' surplus, would require forecasting models of far more sophistication than those currently available.

5. Ports

The lively debate on transport economics has recently been extended to investment in new port facilities. The issue was discussed at length in a theoretical article, as yet unbacked with practical application, by Mr R. O. Goss of the Department of Trade and Industry.[1] Newer technological developments in the shipping industry, notably the tendency to larger ships and the move towards 'containerisation', are securing cost reductions to ship operators which could be further extended given the adaptation of ports, through new investment, to provide faster turn-round facilities. Decisions about the scale of such facilities, based on economic appraisals of the returns in relation to investment costs, are thus required. Mr Goss recognised that the relevant costs are largely internal to port authorities, there being no basic externalities leading to a divergence between private and social interests. In short the aim is to ensure the efficiency of normal commercial operations. It is then argued that this in turn depends on a pricing policy for the use of ports which reflects the marginal costs of port improvements. However, as Mr Goss pointed out in a forceful critique of current practices, port dues are often based on the gross (or net) tonnages of shipping with little relationship between charges and the type of facilities used. To take a specific example, ports may not differentiate closely in their pricing between the use of expensive, quick turn-round berths, and less expensive and slower systems. The benefits to shipowners, and ultimately in competitive conditions to their customers, would thus not be reflected in the accounts of port authorities, with a resulting danger of under-investment in technological improvements. Mr Goss therefore recommended as a matter of urgency that research into port costs, which like those of the railways are particularly complex, be undertaken so that a reformed pricing system might be introduced.

To economists this is a familiar argument difficult to resist. It is nothing more than an application of optimum pricing rules. The problem Mr Goss foresaw is essentially a practical one depending on the apparent difficulties of isolating costs effectively and making the necessary reforms in charging systems. While this would be his first priority he went on to argue that the desired changes would take considerable time, whereas investment decisions are required in the very near future. Therefore he recommended that cost-benefit methods of appraisal be used in the interim

[1] 'Towards an Economic Appraisal of Port Investments', *Journal of Transport Economics and Policy*, September 1967.

period (presumably by the Department of Trade and Industry or the National Ports Council) to investigate the values likely to be generated by new installations. The 'benefits', which are difficult to measure, would be assessed on 'shadow values' derived from detailed studies of the economics of ship operation,[1] and of the reduction in costs which might be forthcoming. The proposal, in short, is that shadow pricing, a familiar piece of cost-benefit methodology, should be used as an immediate planning tool essentially as a second-best alternative to reform of the port pricing system.

Without evidence on the practicability and accuracy of the shadow-pricing devices to be adopted it is, of course, difficult to comment further on Mr Goss's suggestions. His article was interesting, first, as a critique of pricing practices which have received little attention from economists and, secondly, as an example of the conflicts which can arise between the 'pricing' and 'cost-benefit' schools of thought. In an area where externalities and group wants are absent and where commercial and social interests do not therefore conflict, one's predilections would favour the former alternative.

6. Research and development

It is often urged that attempts should be made to quantify the benefits flowing from government sponsorship of research and development activities.[2] Here progress has been extremely slow, no doubt because such attempts enter the realms of the unknown and the unquantifiable. So often large-scale projects of dubious commercial validity are defended on grounds of technological spillovers that it seems appropriate to make a start on *ex post* appraisal. This has been attempted by Messrs K. Grossfield and J. B. Heath for the modest case of the development of an improved potato-harvesting machine undertaken by the National Research and Development Corporation.[3] They pointed out that

'it would have been a lucky shot indeed to have estimated at the appropriate (decision-making) times in the past the present value of the prospective stream of net social benefits'.

Their aim was to estimate the gain to farmers in the form of cost-savings from the superior machine (given their belief that the active participation of the NRDC speeded up the development process by two years). The gains were shown to exceed the costs of development, including one development failure, and of scrapping a model. The authors offered the result as some justification for a public body which

---

[1] A specific study is in R. O. Goss, 'The Turnround of Cargo Liners and its Effect on Sea Transport Costs', *Journal of Transport Economics and Policy,* January 1967.
[2] A short incisive critique is in Professor John Jewkes's Wincott Memorial Lecture, *Government and High Technology,* Occasional Paper 37, IEA, 1972.
[3] 'The Benefit and Cost of Government Support for Research and Development', *Economic Journal,* September 1966.

actively attempts to speed up development in selected cases. Unfortunately other workers have also been unable to estimate the value of technological innovation and the subject remains characterised by special pleading rather than by analytical precision.[1]

7. The nationalised industries

There has so far been no explicit mention of the nationalised industries in this *Paper*. Products are sold in the market and 'externality' effects are not normally considered. But in some instances, notably electricity generation, there are 'production-to-production' effects and indivisibilities. Acute problems also arise because investments in the public sector vary in capital intensity. Classic instances are the comparative capital cost of electricity generation in conventional and nuclear-powered installations, and of electrified and diesel-powered rail services. Further difficulties result from technical progress. Given the long life of the assets it is all too easy, in comparing the merits of alternative modes of supply, to find the original calculations upset by new discoveries. As Professor Williams observed, some of the choices between installing nuclear and conventional power stations amazingly failed to take into account that technical progress was possible in both.[2]

Cost-benefit appraisals in such cases are more akin to those in private sector investment decisions; they are less closely linked to examples in which externality and collectivity difficulties are important. The similarities in the approaches derive from the highly technical controversies on techniques of final appraisal. For example, the choice between the 'internal rate of return' and the 'present value' approaches has an important bearing on the appropriate criteria to adopt in planning investments,[3] and considerable interest has been shown in finding an appropriate 'trial rate of discount' for investment appraisal.[4]

[1] A. L. R. Nicholson, 'The Practical Application of Cost-Benefit Analysis to R and D Investment Decisions', in M. G. Kendall (ed.), *Cost-Benefit Analysis,* English Universities Press, 1971, is able to quote only one other case-study similar to that of Messrs. Grossfield and Heath. P. K. Woolley, 'A Cost-Benefit Analysis ·of the Concorde Project', *Journal of Transport Economics and Policy,* September 1972, is also unable to place a value on R and D benefits.

[2] *Economics in Unwonted Places, loc. cit.* The important French experience in electricity planning is summarised by R. L. Meek, 'The Allocation of Expenditure in the Electricity Supply Industry', in Peacock and Robertson, *op. cit.*

[3] Ralph Turvey, *loc. cit.*

[4] A trial rate of discount of 8 per cent (based on what was believed to represent the opportunity cost of capital) was proposed in the White Paper on *Economic and Financial Obligations of the Nationalised Industries,* Cmnd. 3437, HMSO, November 1967. It was criticised as being too low an estimate by A. M. Alfred, 'The Correct Yardstick for State Investment', *District Bank Review,* June 1968. By 1973 the rate stood at 10 per cent. A discussion of returns is in G. Polanyi, *Comparative Returns from Investment in Nationalised Industries,* Background Memorandum 1, IEA, 1968. His pessimistic views on cost-benefit analysis are in pp. 9-13.

VI Summary and Conclusions

SUMMARY

1. The essence of an economic appraisal of any course of action lies in setting the total value of benefits against the total costs. This is the type of exercise in which business is constantly engaged, the benefits and costs being reflected *via* the price mechanism through the workings of the market forces of supply and demand as they affect the prices received for goods sold and costs of factors of production. In some circumstances market forces may fail to reflect all costs and benefits—the foundation of the distinction between private and social costs and benefits. The extent to which this defect in the private sector should be considered as serious is under constant dispute. In some cases (road congestion, industrial location, pollution control) divergence might be corrected by suitable market-influencing or market-creating actions. Measurement difficulties must be emphasised.

2. Investment appraisal through some form of cost-benefit analysis, when the external effects of private actions are substantial and it is difficult or impossible to collect payment, may be essential while the belief that it should be applied to government schemes is overdue evidence of a desire to bring public spending under closer scrutiny. The White Paper of February 1966[1] mentioned the need to develop 'better methods to measure and compare the cost-effectiveness of alternative courses of action' in the planning of 'economic services' (including transport, the nationalised industries and defence), adding that 'analogous opportunities exist for application in social and community services'. A number of Ministries have actively sponsored cost-benefit studies, and 'output budgeting'[2] techniques are attracting increasing attention. Development of the subject has also revitalised discussion in whole areas of economic science, most notably in the somewhat sterile field of welfare economics hitherto characterised by subtle but basically unquantified argument. Specialists in public finance are also turning their interest increasingly towards the results of public expenditure in terms of value to the community rather than debating costs and 'what can be afforded', important though these remain.

[1] *Public Expenditure: Planning and Control,* Cmnd. 2915, HMSO, February 1966.
[2] The phrase, due to C. J. Hitch, first defence controller under Mr Robert Macnamara in the Kennedy/Johnson administration, is American. It has been brought into British circulation by Peter Jay (*The Times,* 6 and 13 June, 1968), an advocate of cost-benefit and cost-effectiveness studies.

3. Cost-benefit studies may be unsatisfactory because of the quantification un-certainties associated with the elusive and entangled web of the direct and indirect effects to be measured. The usefulness of cost-benefit analysis is critically dependent on the realism of the valuation assumptions. How firmly based are they on the preferences of individuals as expressed through organised markets? To what extent are they arbitrarily determined by the analysts' value-judgements? There is a clear danger, in some examples, of excesses of enthusiasm leading to attempts to value benefits in monetary terms despite all available methods of shadow pricing being misleading and hence either inaccurate or incomplete.[1] In other examples—the Roskill Report provides an excellent case study—a gap in measurement (that of a broad range of environmental and regional planning considerations) simply opened the floodgates of controversy. The device of constructing 'scales of effectiveness', for use when monetary appraisal proves impossible, may be insecurely based on the somewhat arbitrary views of the investigators.

4. Severe difficulties also surround the use of the 'rates of return' or 'discounted present values' which are the end-product of a thorough-going cost-benefit appraisal. Apart from the fundamental controversy over the relative merits of the opportunity cost of capital and the social rate of time preference as the basis for a 'cut-off' criterion, the specialists are not agreed that the derived cost-benefit rate of return can be compared with other rates. This issue is crucial in road investments.

5. In addition there is the thorny issue of distribution of benefits, or of costs, among the income groups within the population. Most analyses assume that a pound's worth of benefit is counted as one pound regardless of the income of the recipient. The aim is to choose projects which maximise national product or national satisfaction.[2] Yet government projects may have ends in view other than 'efficiency': they may aim to alter the income distribution between classes of people (class being defined variously as income category, area of residence, age or some other variable). How are high-yield projects with 'adverse' income distributional effects to be assessed against lower-yielding projects with more 'favourable' income effects? The traditional view is that efficiency should be maximised and side-effects on income distribution handled *via* the machinery of taxation and redistribution, blunt weapons

---

[1] At this stage the reader may have asked himself whether *ex-post* checks have been made on valuation results. In one example it was shown that the non-market benefits in American water resource studies have sometimes been seriously over-stated: R. H. Haveman, *The Economic Performance of Public Investments*, Johns Hopkins University Press, London, 1972. The writer argues that basic improvement in valuation techniques represents a higher priority than the sophisticated theorising so often apparent in cost-benefit work.

[2] National satisfaction rather than national product since the latter, as conventionally measured, will exclude non-market benefits or reflect them only *via* the factor cost of provision.

though they may at present be. Professors B. Weisbrod[1] and A. Maas[2] have questioned this approach. The former argues that cost-benefit studies should wherever possible list benefits by class of recipient to give an immediate impression of the scheme under review. At a more sophisticated level he suggests a weighting system for reducing the range of distributional benefits to a single common measure. The proposal, very similar to the thinking of Professor Maas, is based on the supposition that many schemes may have been shelved during the legislative process despite their high benefit-cost ratios because of supposed distributional effects. With sufficient experience of the preferences (or 'trade-off' rate) of elected representatives between efficiency and distribution, Professors Weisbrod and Maas were optimistic that a scheme for explicitly incorporating distributional features could be formalised within the analytical framework of cost-benefit appraisal.[3] But both emphasised that 'trade-off' analysis was still in its infancy.

CONCLUSIONS

1. Blanket approval or condemnation of cost-benefit methodology is impossible. Much depends on technical and economic considerations relevant to any area of potential application. Whatever else may be said about it, there is no doubt that the effort of making a cost-benefit study concentrates attention on basic issues. The task of listing relevant costs and benefits is in itself a valuable discipline. But because cost-benefit analysis, almost by definition, must encounter difficulties of quantification it cannot be regarded as a technique which can simply be 'switched on' in the hope that it will provide an unequivocal solution to a problem.

2. Some economists have argued that a distinction can be made between two aspects of allocating resources. The total sum it is economically efficient to spend in various broad classes of use is one. Unfortunately in planning government expenditure, inter-sectoral decisions require choices between heterogeneous and often *non-comparable* ranges of benefit (health versus education, versus roads, versus defence, and so on) which cannot easily be handled by cost-benefit methods. But, given a sum to be spent under each head arrived at (say) by political decisions, its allocation

[1] 'Income Redistribution Effects and Cost Benefit Analysis', in Samuel B. Chase, Jnr. (ed.), *Problems in Public Expenditure Analysis*. The Brookings Institution, Washington DC, 1968. This is the report of a conference organised as a follow-up to a meeting with proceedings edited by R. Dorfman (below, p. 72). The American Bureau of the Budget was instrumental in organising both sets of discussions.

[2] 'Benefit-Cost Analysis: Its Relevance to Public Investment Decisions', *Quarterly Journal of Economics*, May 1966.

[3] Attempts to analyse the social preferences thrown up by legislative and democratic processes are becoming more common among American writers. The literature is summarised by Baumol (*op. cit.*). Major works are J. M. Buchanan and G. Tullock, *The Calculus of Consent*, University of Michigan, Ann Arbor, 1962; G. Tullock, *Towards a Mathematics of Politics*, University of Michigan, Ann Arbor, 1966, and *Private Wants, Public Means*, Basic Books, New York, 1970.

between alternative *projects* may be aided by cost-benefit appraisals. This is a lower level but potentially fruitful avenue for use of the technique.[1]

3. Since cost-benefit analysis is an imperfect tool it must be asked whether more effective guide-lines for public action can be discovered. Does the government have to provide so many services on a 'public goods' basis? Could market provision be effectively organised, say, in health or education, with vouchers used to ensure that services are available to all and overcome initial problems of unequal incomes? Could market research and opinion sampling methods be developed to guide the supply of community services and indicate the nature of households' preferences? Is road pricing (despite its reliance on estimates of external congestion costs) a more fruitful avenue of approach than attempts to measure the benefits of road improvement indirectly? In many activities 'the market' has simply been ousted as an allocative mechanism—but once that happens, and no matter how cogent the reasons may appear, the task of choice and allocation remains. There can be no clear presumption that public provision, guided by cost-benefit study, is necessarily superior to alternative arrangements.

4. The last word on cost-benefit analysis is best left with the leading American economist, Professor Robert Dorfman. In his introduction to a Brookings Institution symposium he records that in the course of discussion many administrators were hopeful that the approach might help them to make difficult allocation decisions. On the other hand, some practitioners of the art of cost-benefit analysis likened the problem to appraising the quality of a horse and rabbit stew, the rabbit being those consequences that could be measured and evaluated numerically, and the horse

'the amalgam of external effects, social, emotional and psychological impacts and historical and aesthetic considerations that can be adjudged only roughly and subjectively'.[2]

Since the horse was bound to dominate the flavour of the stew, meticulous evaluation of the rabbit would hardly seem worthwhile.

Though this parable was cautionary rather than an obituary notice for cost-benefit analysis, eulogising the technique as the latest and hence the greatest discovery of pure science is nonetheless foolhardy.

[1] The points in this paragraph derive largely from comments by Mr D. L. Munby, Professor J. Wiseman and Professor J. R. Sargent in evidence to the *Select Committee on Nationalised Industries: Sub-Committee A, Minutes of Evidence*, 26 July, 1967, HMSO, 1967, 440-xiii; and by Mr N. Scott, 'The Planning and Cost-Benefit Analysis of Social Investments', *International Institute of Labour Studies Bulletin*, No. 2, February 1967. It is interesting to note that in his evidence Professor Wiseman insisted on the dangers inherent in nationalised industries seeking to justify non-commercial behaviour on grounds of social benefit. He foresaw a tendency for 'the benefits to be equated to the deficit' with consequential damage to managerial efficiency. He did not regard external social costs as unimportant, urging instead that nationalised industries should be subjected to the same kind of centrally-determined rules and constraints on social benefit and cost problems as other enterprises.

[2] R. Dorfman (ed.), *Measuring Benefits of Government Investments*, The Brookings Institution, Washington DC, 1965, p. 2. This volume covers a number of applications of cost-benefit analysis.

Further Reading

The reader will appreciate that examples of cost-benefit analysis can be drawn from many industries and activities. There are thus very few references which span the whole range of issues involved. An outstanding survey, containing a comprehensive bibliography of 90 references, is:

Prest, A. R., and Turvey, Ralph, 'Cost-Benefit Analysis: A Survey', *Economic Journal,* Vol. LXXV, No. 300, December 1965.

The paper is reprinted in:

American Economic Association—Royal Economic Society, *Surveys of Economic Theory: Volume III. Resource Allocation,* Macmillan, London, 1966, and in Richard Layard (ed.), *Cost-Benefit Analysis,* Penguin Modern Economics Readings, Penguin Books, 1972.

The latter contains a useful summary article by the editor, a mass of bibliographical material, and reprints of other important papers (some very difficult).

Useful collections of case studies drawn from a wide area are contained in:

Dorfman, R. (ed.), *Measuring Benefits of Government Investments,* Brookings Institution, Washington DC, 1965.

Chase, Samuel B., Jnr. (ed.), *Problems in Public Expenditure Analysis* Brookings Institution, Washington DC, 1968.

Readers primarily interested in transport questions can consult:

Foster, C.D., *The Transport Problem*, Blackie, London, 1963.

The theory of cost-benefit analysis, in particular its relationship to welfare economics, is treated in three textbooks. In order of difficulty they are:

Pearce, D. W., *Cost-Benefit Analysis*, Macmillan Studies in Economics, London, 1971.

Dasgupta, A. K., and Pearce, D. W., *Cost-Benefit Analysis, Theory and Practice,* Macmillan, London, 1972.

Mishan, E. J., *Cost-Benefit Analysis, An Informal Introduction,* Allen and Unwin, London, 1971.

There is similar useful material in:

Millward, R., *Public Expenditure Economics,* McGraw-Hill, London, 1971.

The general problem of central government expenditure, with particularly useful chapters by Professors Jack Wiseman and R. L. Meek, is covered by:

Robertson, D. J., and Peacock, A. T. (eds.), *Public Expenditure, Appraisal and Control,* Oliver and Boyd, Edinburgh, 1963.

A wide-ranging discussion of externality problems is to be found in:

Mishan, E. J., *The Costs of Economic Growth,* Staples Press, London, 1967.

IEA Publications

SUBSCRIPTION SERVICE

An annual subscription to the IEA ensures that all regular series, research studies, etc., are sent without further charge immediately on publication – representing a substantial saving.

The cost (including postage) is £10·00 (£7·50 for teachers and students) for twelve months (£9·50 if by Banker's Order); US $25 or equivalent for overseas subscriptions.

To: The Treasurer,
  Institute of Economic Affairs,
  2 Lord North Street,
  Westminster,
  London SW1P 3LB

Please register a subscription of £10·00 (£7·50 for teachers and bona fide students) for the twelve months beginning..

☐ Remittance enclosed   ☐ Please send invoice

☐ I should prefer to pay by Banker's Order which reduces the subscription to £9·50.

Name ....

Address ....

....

Position ....

Signed..

Date ....

IEA READINGS in print

1. Education—A Framework for Choice

A. C. F. BEALES, MARK BLAUG, E. G. WEST,
SIR DOUGLAS VEALE, *with an appraisal by* DR. RHODES BOYSON.
Second Edition, 1970 (90p)

2. Growth through Industry

JOHN JEWKES, JACK WISEMAN, RALPH HARRIS, JOHN BRUNNER, RICHARD
LYNN, and seven company chairmen. 1967 (£1·00)

4. Taxation—A Radical Approach

VITO TANZI, J. B. BRACEWELL-MILNES, D. R. MYDDLETON. 1970 (90p)

5. Economic Issues in Immigration

CHARLES WILSON, W. H. HUTT, SUDHA SHENOY, DAVID COLLARD,
E. J. MISHAN, GRAHAM HALLETT, *with an Introduction by* SIR ARNOLD
PLANT. 1970 (£1·25)

7. Verdict on Rent Control

F. A HAYEK, MILTON FRIEDMAN and GEORGE J. STIGLER, BERTRAND
DE JOUVENEL, F. W. PAISH, SVEN RYDENFELT, *with an introduction by*
F. G. PENNANCE. 1972 (£1.00)

10. Mergers, Take-overs and the Structure of Industry

G. C. ALLEN, M. E. BEESLEY, HAROLD EDEY, BRIAN HINDLEY, SIR
ANTHONY BURNEY, PETER CANNON, IAN FRASER, LORD SHAWCROSS,
SIR GEOFFREY HOWE, LORD ROBBINS. 1973 (£1.00)

11. Regional Policy for Ever?

GRAHAM HALLETT, PETER RANDALL, E. G. WEST. 1973 (£1·80)

12. The Economics of Charity

ARMEN A. ALCHIAN and WILLIAM R. ALLEN, MICHAEL H. COOPER,
ANTHONY J. CULYER, MARILYN J. IRELAND, THOMAS R. IRELAND,
DAVID B. JOHNSON, JAMES KOCH, A. J. SALSBURY, GORDON TULLOCK.
1974 (£2·00)

13. Government and the Land

A. A. WALTERS, F. G. PENNANCE, W. A. WEST, D. R. DENMAN,
BARRY BRACEWELL-MILNES, S. E. DENMAN, D. G. SLOUGH,
STUART INGRAM. 1974 (£1·00)

76